WARNING SIGNS

WARNING SIGNS
A Guidebook for Parents

How to read the early signals of low self-esteem,
addiction, and hidden violence in your kids

JOHN KELLY
Executive and Clinical Director of ExtraCare Health Services

WITH BRIAN J. KAREM

LifeLine
Press

Washington, D.C.

Library of Congress Cataloging-in-Publication Data

Kelly, John.
 Warning signs : how to read the early signals of low self-esteem and addiction in your kids / John Kelly and Brian Karem.
    p. ; cm.
Includes bibliographical references and index.
 ISBN 0-89526-189-8 (acid-free paper)

 [DNLM: 1. Behavior, Addictive--psychology--Popular Works. 2. Parent-Child Relations--Popular Works. 3. Parenting--psychology--Popular Works. 4. Self Concept--Popular Works. WM 176 K29w 2002] I. Karem, Brian. II. Title.

  618.92'86--dc21

2002000957

Published in the United States by
LifeLine Press
A Regnery Publishing Company
One Massachusetts Avenue, NW
Washington, DC 20001

Visit us at www.lifelinepress.com

Distributed to the trade by
National Book Network
4720-A Boston Way
Lanham, MD 20706

Printed on acid-free paper
Manufactured in the United States of America
Design by Marja Walker

10 9 8 7 6 5 4 3 2 1

Books are available in quantity for promotional or premium use. Write to Director of Special Sales, Regnery Publishing, Inc., One Massachusetts Avenue, NW, Washington, DC 20001, for information on discounts and terms or call (202) 216-0600.

CONTENTS

PREFACE

AFTER FIFTEEN YEARS OF RESEARCHING backgrounds and counseling substance abusers, co-dependents, gamblers, and children of alcoholics, I found what I believe is the common denominator and root cause of addictive illness. It is low self-esteem.

It begins to manifest itself in children at an early age. If we take into consideration that the two fundamental building blocks for self-esteem are confidence and self-respect it is easy to see how a child growing up in a dysfunctional family (or feeling a lack of self-respect or confidence for any reason) can fall victim to this disease. Low self-esteem is a disease common to those who engage in substance abuse or compulsive gambling, or fall victim to child abuse. It is a disease that is eroding this country's most vital foundation—the family. In fact, I believe that it is this country's largest health problem. Before church or government was created, the family was an institution already in place and it is threatened today by our ignorance and misplaced thinking.

It may be hard, at first glance, to understand why low self-esteem is a disease. But taking a look at the definition of the word disease in Webster's *New World Dictionary*, you read that a disease is: "any departure from health and wellness in general, or a particular destruction process in an organism." This certainly covers low self-esteem. You can separate the word by its syllables and see that someone suffering from low self-esteem is certainly in a state of dis-ease.

In this book you will learn how to identify low self-esteem in your child and you'll learn how to intervene and stop it before it progresses into substance abuse, compulsive gambling, addictive illness, or depression. If your child has already progressed into any of these situations, this book will show you how to intervene on these self-destructive behaviors and obtain the correct treatment for your child. You will also learn how to build self-worth in your child using empowering techniques that will help them become successful and healthy adults. The appropriate type of treatment is extremely important for your child if he or she is already abusing substances. The appropriate treatment means a specific, individualized treatment approach that is right for your child.

For years treatment in the substance abuse field has mainly consisted of a cookie-cutter approach or a one-size-fits-all treatment. For instance, there is a major emphasis on group counseling, which was initiated by the success of Alcoholics Anonymous—a group that has been successful in helping a small population of those suffering from addictive illness. And, personally, I can't thank Narcotics Anonymous enough for the spiritual gifts given to me over the years in working toward my own recovery. However, even though I believe addiction treatment facilities, whether they be inpatient or outpatient, have the well-being of the client in mind, there have been some large glitches in the one-size-fits-all treatment approach. In any twelve-step group approach, desire is the key ingredient—the desire to stop using the substance and to attend a meeting. The underlying theory is, "Bring the body and the mind will follow." When the effort sometimes fails, because the abuser lacks the desire, then the old rationale is best expressed by the even older cliché, "They're not ready yet."

This logic fails on adults and children alike. Children, especially, often don't have the life experiences that create the desire to overcome the problems of their abuse. Many adolescents, teenagers, or young adults labor under the misconception of immortality, or at least act as if they have as much belief in it as in God.

But many of us in the field have nevertheless been trained to believe that if someone doesn't respond to the traditional ideas, then "they're just not ready yet." Early on in my counseling internship in an inner city hospital, I unfortunately also fell victim to that philosophy—as did all of my colleagues. Who was I to think that every individual who came through our unit should react positively to group counseling, to embrace Alcoholics Anonymous or Narcotics Anonymous meetings and display a desire to embrace recovery? Well, it would have made my life easier, but the truth was far from the ideal. We had abundant examples of patients who didn't show enough desire even to obey the rules and regulations of the unit, much less to get clean and sober.

Patients on the unit were also extremely different in their likes and dislikes in regard to food, hairstyles, clothing, music, relationships, prejudices, etc. They all had their specific "drug of choice" or perhaps unique drug combination. With all of this taken into consideration I soon found myself wondering why we should believe that one type of medical treatment would serve everyone who came to us with an addictive illness. Just as an oncologist prescribes different treatments for each cancer patient, so must we treat each person individually who comes to us with an abuse problem.

Now, consider psychotherapy. Does every client do well with cognitive therapy, or behavior therapy, or psychodynamic, reality, or family therapy? Of course not. The reason there are so many different therapies is because every person is a unique individual, and a therapy that might work well for one person may not be at all suitable for another. That is why the cookie-cutter approach has worked for the minority, not the majority, of abuse patients. Another factor that has fueled this group approach is money. It is obviously much more profitable for a treatment facility to hire one counselor to provide group therapy for twelve or more patients in one session several times a day—and then charge insurance companies and HMOs per patient—than to hire one counselor to meet individually with only six or so patients a day. This has become very profitable, but brings few results and has been attacked by the insurance companies as well as the managed care providers.

Please understand that I believe in group therapy and how vital it can be for the appropriate patients. What I do not agree with is group therapy exclusively for each patient. For example, an asocial or antisocial individual obviously will not do very well in a group setting. Borderline substance abusers also typically do not do well in groups. Also, we must take into consideration a patient suffering from some type of physical, sexual, or emotional trauma who has problems with trust. Will they share their deepest and darkest secrets (which often are the root cause of their low self-esteem and addiction problems) with a group of complete strangers? Even in the twelve-step community that emphasizes anonymity there is a saying, "If you don't want it said outside the rooms, don't say it in the rooms."

The alternative to group treatment is an individualized treatment program that's designed specifically for each person. In this book we hope to acquaint you with the tools to treat your children yourself and hopefully to stop problems before they start. We will talk about specific gender counseling, building rapport and trust, discipline, and of course parental education and family education. Finally, and most importantly, we place a strong emphasis on building self-esteem through helping the children become confident and by helping them focus on their self-*respect* and not self-*destruction*. This is our approach at our facility, the ExtraCare Counseling Centers.

Through it all we have tried to live by the words of Walter Elias Disney, "America's greatest resource is the minds of its children."

With that said, I would like to thank the following individuals for making this book possible. First I would like to thank God for enlightening me with the wisdom and the gift of common sense that has empowered me to be a positive influence in the recovery process for countless clients and their families. I also want to thank Fr.

Rodney Crues for his encouragement to enter the substance abuse field, along with my mentor, Fr. Dennis Mansmann, who not only had faith in me and gave me my first job in the field, but who also encouraged my work and research and was always available to me for professional guidance and personal counseling. In fact, if not for Father Mansmann, I doubt if ExtraCare would exist, much less this book. I would also like to thank my teachers, by whom I had the honor of being supervised over the years: Dr. Jerome Gordon, who specialized in Gestalt and cognitive behavior therapy and gave me my first insight into low self-esteem and how destructive it can be; Dr. James O'Connell, who made me see how important behavioral therapy is; Dr. Michael Horowitz, who specialized in psychoanalytical therapy; and Dr. Edward Merski, who has educated me on psychodynamic and family therapy. My thanks also to Stephen Altman, Esq., friend and confidant, and Zion Lutheran Church of Rahway, New Jersey, especially Pastor Linderman, who gave us free space to counsel our clients and do our research.

It is important to note here that for those who suffer from biological disorders such as manic-depression or schizophrenia, self-esteem is not the root cause of these disorders.

Most importantly I thank my wife, Marilyn, who spent countless hours typing my first manuscript and editing my research, and had faith in me and my ideas and encouraged my dream when ExtraCare Health Services began with one client in 1988. And please indulge me as I thank my invaluable colleagues who make up our professional team at ExtraCare: Roger Boyle, Melinda Judd, Vincent Rumain, Veronica Mullin, Ruth Moore, Marilyn McCusker, and Leo Battenhausen. Thanks, guys, for blessing me and our clients with your excellent clinical work. I also want to thank Brian Karem for believing in my philosophy and helping me write a great book.

—*John Kelly, June 1, 2001*

INTRODUCTION

LET ME FIRST SAY THAT I HAVE ABSOLUTELY NO EXPERIENCE in the field of substance abuse, low self-esteem, or depression other than what I have gained by living life, being a parent, a husband, and a friend.

I have, for the most part, covered crime and politics most of my adult life. Yes, I've heard the joke that the two are often the same, and actually the observation isn't that far removed from reality. So, I agreed to take on this project, curious about John's ideas and, as a reporter, skeptical of quick fixes or any fixes that might work.

But a funny thing happened. As I got more and more involved in this book, I began to see what John was talking about, applied it to my own life, and began to see the patterns that he had spotted in other lives. As a crime reporter I have interviewed dozens if not hundreds of inmates in prison. Many of them had little in common, but I'd venture to say that 99 percent of them did have one remarkable thing in common: either there were no fathers in their lives or the fathers were abusive, neglectful, or both. I had often used this observation in arguing about the need for parents to be parents to their children.

When not working as a reporter, I have been a Sunday School teacher and a football, soccer, basketball, and baseball coach. I have helped teachers at public schools on field trips and have spent a good deal of my spare time either teaching or assisting children in some form ever since my own children were toddlers. I do this because it's what my own father did. I also do this because I like spending time with my children.

I say this because I have learned something through my association with John and I hope other parents do too. I have become more cognizant of my own behavior and how what I do affects my children. I have come to see that the people I enjoy most in life are those who've never forgotten what it was to be a child and yet, at the same time, those very people are among the most mature I've ever met.

I have often said that I've made a lot of decisions in my life and I cannot be sure if all of them were right, but the one I've never questioned was my decision to marry my wife. She is the center of my universe, along with my children.

John helped me feel great about all that and I get a renewed sense of accomplishment every time I look at my children and feel joyous over the decisions that they have made. I hope, in some small way, I've helped them become better human beings.

My father died of cancer and I took care of him during the last eight months of his illness. The night he died I held his hand. I hope I did right by him too. I remember for many years being estranged from my father. We didn't get along and we didn't spend much time together. That ended long before he got sick, and I was happy to have had ten good years with him in a very close relationship.

But two things that happened with my father remind me of why I took on this project with John. The first occurred one night in San Antonio, Texas. I was a reporter at a local television station and my father came to visit. We sat in a pub one night with a few friends and I remember my father just sitting and grinning. "What's up, Pop?" I asked. He explained to me the joy of merely sitting in a bar and having a drink with his oldest son—an activity he had wanted to engage in with his own father, but his mother had made the two feel too guilty ever to try it.

The second thing I remember is when my father got sick with cancer. He was talking about how he resented the chasm that had formed between us many years before, how needlessly he'd wasted the time, and how he wished he could have been close to me during my adolescence and early adulthood.

"It's okay Dad," I said. "That's years in the past and we're here together now."

My father admonished me and said it wasn't okay. He knew he could eventually die from his illness and he told me that family meant everything to him and always had and he hadn't been true to that one ideal. He was heartsick over it and no matter how much I tried to console him, I don't think I ever made him feel right. This stuck with me and I began to think about my own children. At the time I was traveling perhaps 150 to 200 days a year as a correspondent for "America's Most Wanted." I was getting to see the entire country and other countries, but my young sons were without me for a good length of time.

I reassessed my life at that point, for although I was all right with myself and my father, I didn't want to have the regrets he had. I made changes and I've never been happier for them. My father gave me that gift.

Which brings me back to this project. I came to see it as another way to pay homage to my father and to my mother, who struggled to raise four kids after she and my father divorced. I've come to believe, independently of this book, in many of the things John is struggling to convey to parents everywhere in these pages.

For the first time I met someone with the training and knowledge to put into practice and words the ideals I hold most dear when it comes to raising children, and the effect a parent could, should, and needs to have on a child's life.

I remember one time in the late eighties interviewing a fifteen-year-old gang-banger on San Antonio's west side. He had knife wounds all over his body. He'd been shot twice in his young life. He had three children and a wife whom he never saw. He died within six months of the interview and I remember at the time asking him about his own father. He didn't know him. His mother was never around and he and his five brothers and sisters raised themselves. Was it any wonder that his life, and the lives of many others in the San Antonio projects, resembled something from *Lord of the Flies?*

Is there truly any wonder at all why there is so much hate and strife in a world where we do not take care of our children? Perhaps in some small way this book can change that.

For that I am eternally grateful to John Kelly for making me a part of this project and I hope I have paid a debt to my own parents who managed to instill the feeling of family and love in me.

—Brian J. Karem

PART I
SIGNS OF TROUBLE

CHAPTER 1
Underlying causes of addiction

My son stayed out all night and now he just stays in his bedroom and won't come out. Should I be worried?

FROM THE TIME YOU BRING A WRIGGLING, GURGLING MASS of baby flesh home from the hospital until the time you leave this earthly existence, you can be guaranteed that your child will do plenty of things that are going to surprise you.

In early infancy these surprises are usually, and thankfully, limited in a healthy baby. Besides the common bouts with rashes and ear infections, colds and tantrums, a parent may also be greeted with very humbling and potentially embarrassing situations. Older parents have been known to warn younger parents of the problems brought about through the various and sometimes, in retrospect, humorous ways a child can embarrass parents in public—when there is something wrong with the diaper and a crowd around to witness it. No parent alive, young or old, will think twice about the young embarrassed parents trying to clean up an unexpected gift from their young baby in a public setting. Since most of us have been there, we only pray that such accidents occur outdoors.

But by the time the child reaches adolescence the surprises he or she will bring home for the parent are of a much more serious nature than a dirty diaper. Sometimes, a parent who has been loving and committed for a dozen or more years might be greeted with potentially serious surprises, such as drug abuse, addiction, low self-esteem, and/or violent tendencies in their children. If the parent isn't in denial about the big surprise—drug use, for example—then that parent will inevitably wonder if there were other surprises along the way that went unnoticed.

"Did I miss something?" is one of the most natural questions a loving parent can ask.

But the time to wonder if you've missed something is not after a catastrophe has occurred. It's now, prior to any possible catastrophe. Perhaps if your children stayed out all night there is a reasonable explanation, but you need to find out by communicating with them. Then again, after you talk to them, you have to probe their behavior even if it appears everything is all right. Use good, sound common sense and always ask yourself if the situation, the explanation, and your child make sense.

Parents, then, should strive to be alert to anything different or new in their child's behavior. This means logically assessing a child's behavior and looking for subtle clues that point to larger problems. This is not always as easy as it sounds since parents' judgment can be impaired by their proximity, love, and concern for their child. Of course, the opposite may be true as well. A parent can have an impaired judgment because of the distance, lack of concern, and absence of love for their children.

One of our cases at ExtraCare involved a child named Kenny. He was fifteen years old. He kept a passable grade point average, didn't fail any classes, and got up every morning and went to school. His parents later said there was no warning sign for Kenny's problem.

But he was addicted to marijuana. He smoked outside the house with his friends. Sometimes they smoked at school during lunch break. Kenny also smoked marijuana every night at the home of a friend who used the drug with his parents' consent—parents who thought the social use of marijuana was acceptable.

Meanwhile, Kenny's parents just thought he was going over to a friend's house to listen to music. He most certainly was, but to put it in terms many teens from the late '60s through the late '70s would understand, there was a lot of lava lamps, black lights, and incense involved.

Still, Kenny always came home at a decent hour. He remained a well-behaved child, and the only thing the parents noticed out of the ordinary was that he would come home and go up to his room to listen to music in an isolated environment for long periods of time. His parents thought it was normal behavior for a teenager and decided to give the boy his space. Other than that one character misstep there were no outward signs of trouble. Kenny even held down a part-time job working in a book store on Saturdays and appeared to his parents to be an excellent money manager.

But while Kenny always seemed to have money to purchase whatever he wanted, his parents were not involved in Kenny's money management. They did not know that the reason Kenny had so much ready money was because he had branched out into the high-risk, high-drama world of drug dealing.

Kenny's parents thought they were adequately involved in Kenny's life and knew everything they needed to know as parents. All of that changed one fall day when Kenny went out to lunch with his school buddies and decided to detour into a secluded, wooded area behind the high school. When the motley crew returned to their next class, a teacher thought she smelled marijuana smoke on Kenny. At that point, under New Jersey law, the school required Kenny to take a drug test. He tested positive, and only then did the parents become aware of the problem. When Kenny came into treatment, he said he had been smoking and dealing since he was about thirteen; the child's cunning had enabled him to hide it for more than two years.

As for Kenny's parents, they lived a nightmare that most parents dread even considering; you do everything you think you're supposed to do, and more, and something bad still happens to your child. In Kenny's case, his parents didn't have to see their child suffer dire consequences, but that can happen. Getting a phone call that your child has been involved in a fatality is a constant concern of most parents who have teenage children.

While these worst-case scenarios are not common, far more common is **parental denial**. As they say, "denial ain't just a river in Egypt." Many parents simply refuse to admit their children have abuse or addiction problems, and the source for that denial can be as varied as the parents who are engaged in it. Parents can be alert and caring and go into denial when confronted with a nightmare situation like Kenny's or they can be uncaring, distant, or violent, or perhaps drug abusers themselves.

The first indication of denial for the clinician treating a family comes mere moments after the parents arrive in a family treatment facility. Usually some of the first words out of a parent's mouth are an attempt to minimize any possibility of drug or alcohol abuse by his or her child.

"They've only tried it a few times," the parents say. "I know my son isn't addicted," or "My daughter wouldn't do that. She doesn't even hang out with those types of people." Many times parents will say these things to clinicians despite the fact that the family has ended up in family counseling because a child tested positive for drugs in a urine test. We've had them say similar things even after their child has been found in possession of drugs at school or been arrested for drug dealing. This is the very nature of denial. A parent will rationalize, explain away, and believe any excuse for their child's behavior besides the obvious and true one.

Denial can hinder a solution, but parents should also realize it is a self-defense mechanism the mind uses to handle trauma. But denial need not be continuous. Parents can and should reevaluate their thinking toward their children frequently.

With that said, even a healthy self-evaluation can be hindered by the duplicity of a child eager to hide his abuse and addiction. Such children can help keep parents in doubt and in denial. We had a case involving a child named Carlos. His parents initially became concerned when they found him with a joint and he denied it was his. As Carlos explained to his parents, he was merely holding the joint for a friend. The parents, skeptical but unsure, pressed, but Carlos did not seem to be the type to be a drug user.

He had no hygiene problems, his school records were exemplary, and his behavior was otherwise stellar. Ultimately, he convinced his parents to give him the benefit of the doubt—that he was merely holding the drugs for a friend—and so they simply threw the joint away after advising their son not to do such foolish things in the future.

Eight or nine months later, a joint was found in Carlos's shirt pocket when he was involved in a traffic stop by a police officer. He was forwarded to us for a drug evaluation. When I had the parents come in with Carlos, which is our protocol, I found they were deep in denial. There was no way, they were sure, that Carlos was involved in drugs.

They candidly discussed the previous incident and how they had evaluated their son for suspected drug behavior. They also talked openly about being convinced their son was innocent. They cited his exemplary behavior and said he was very close to being an honor student. They were so convinced that our investigation was unwarranted that they not only asked us to drop it, but to send a letter to authorities and school officials stating Carlos had no drug problem.

Instead, according to protocol, we did a ten-panel urine drug screen test on Carlos and it came back positive for heroin, marijuana, and cocaine, as well as Xanax. We showed it to the parents, who initially didn't want to believe their child had done anything wrong. But the evidence in black and white quickly led to a major shift in the parents' thinking. They came to realize Carlos had a problem, and ultimately Carlos confessed to using all of the drugs. He even supplied his own evidence of the abuse and addiction by pulling up his sleeves and displaying his needle track marks to his very surprised parents. For some angry children, this behavior has a purpose—to shock and enrage the parent they are mad at. But in Carlos's case, it simply confirmed his abuse.

Carlos added to his parents' surprise when he then confessed he had been a low-level drug dealer, despite all evidence the parents had obtained to the contrary. This kicked off a sixteen-week intensive outpatient program. Amazingly, Carlos cleaned up quickly and well. He was able to stay away from the drug trade and went on to excel in school, graduating from high school on the honor roll. He then went off to college and for more than a year and a half did well scholastically in the university environment.

Last Christmas Carlos's mother called in tears. She and her husband had gone away briefly for the Christmas break. After a year and a half of struggling with Carlos, they felt they had earned some time to themselves and they believed Carlos had progressed enough to take care of himself while they were away. But when the parents came home, they found Carlos lying in their home dead of a heroin overdose.

Carlos's case illustrates not only the problems of denial and deception, but also of relapsing into old, familiar, and self-destructive habits. *Denial, deception, and relapsing behavior are all symptomatic of addiction or abuse and are warning signs for an alert parent.*

An over-reactive parent is also a problem, but rarely will such a parent cause a child to take on the self-destructive habits of addiction if the child has good self-esteem. However, when an over-reactive parent is dealing with a child of low self-esteem, it can have a profound impact on a child, leading to abuse or addiction—or worse in far darker cases. We will cover those issues in greater depth later.

What we usually find at our facility are apathetic parents. These parents are not alert to their children's needs nor are they apt to pick up on any warning signs. Their children in many cases are nothing more than roommates or strangers inhabiting the same home. For whatever reason, and there are as many reasons as there are apathetic parents, these parents put no importance on being close to their children.

Many times the reasons for apathy seem valid to the apathetic parent. They are not apathetic in their own eyes, but merely inundated with the demands of everyday life. They have taken primary focus in their life off of their children and put it onto something else—sometimes justifying such action by saying to themselves they want to do right by their children. "I'm not home with my kids because I have to earn a living," is one such justifiable action. Even so, for many children, latch-key living can be a breeding ground for trouble.

Children will quickly sense and react to this change in focus. Children not only sense the lack of parental involvement in their life, but are usually damaged by it. From their earliest memories they feel no self-worth because of the lack of parental involvement, which in many cases amounts to parental neglect. We have also seen other reasons for parental apathy. Some parents just don't care what their children do, and others believe their children have earned a "free rein." To a child a "free rein" is another word for apathy.

ALERT PARENTAL REMINDER
TO SOME CHILDREN: FREE REIN = APATHY

Do not give your child the mistaken impression you are apathetic to them. Be involved in your child's life and beware of what you say, as well as what you don't say, and beware of how a child may interpret it. Mixed communication signals can have unpleasant results. Make sure when you reward your children with the easing of parental restrictions, that you explain to them that that is in fact what you are doing. Do not give the child the opportunity to mistake it for apathy. As always, do not try to deceive them. In a counseling environment we try to leave no room for interpreting what we say other than how we mean it. You must be explicit and direct with children.

But even while doing so, alert parents can be mistaken for apathetic parents. Indeed, no one is perfect, and at times being tired, rundown, or just inundated with the problems of life can cause even the most alert parent to show signs of apathy. Children, many of whom grasp at the slightest signs of a problem and can misinterpret them, can interpret exhaustion, preoccupation with paying bills, business travel, problems at work, and so on as apathy toward them. Take the time to explain to your children that this is not the case. Today's children, much more plugged in than their parents, need communication, and today's parents, who may have been taught differently by their own parents, need to get used to trying to make their children understand what is going on within the family that affects them. This is not to say that a parent needs to go over the details of the family budget, but when tired and rundown, or just exhausted, it does not hurt to say to a child, "Not now. I care about your problem and I care about you, but right now I need to rest."

The most typical candidate for an apathetic parent is the single mother. Usually, she's the family's sole provider, parent, nurturer, and disciplinarian. She is multiethnic and from multieconomic conditions. She is often of American heritage, rather than a first-generation immigrant.

Like parents in denial, many apathetic parents become aware of a child's drug problem only after a significant "event" connected to the problem comes to the parent's attention—for example, a police intervention. Another first-time "event" that can trigger an apathetic parent's awareness is a telephone call from a guidance counselor or principal at the child's school. Arrests, automobile accidents, or law enforcement "drug sweeps" of street dealers can also be the first indication of the child's enthusiasm for self-destructive, illicit, and addictive behavior.

The bottom line in dealing with parental apathy is to understand that the parent doesn't care, doesn't seem to have time for, or doesn't know that an adolescent child needs clear, definable boundaries. Without the boundaries, some children begin to have feelings of low self-worth and that, in turn, can spiral into abuse, addiction, and even far more drastic behavior.

One case that comes to mind is that of a fifteen-year-old girl named Marie. She came from a family that didn't really care what Marie did as long as things in the home remained quiet. Her parents didn't care what time she came home at night nor with whom she socialized. Just so long as no one rocked the boat, the parents were fine.

But Marie wasn't. She began ditching school, which caused the school administrators to call the parents and put them on the spot. They responded by promising to make Marie attend classes regularly. When she finally showed up in school after missing several weeks, a teacher thought Marie looked despondent and "strung out," so she recommended a drug test to the school's substance abuse coordinator. Marie's urine tested positive for amphetamines and marijuana. That landed Marie and her family at our agency, where they came to be evaluated so Marie could be readmitted to school.

In our initial interview Marie was very belligerent and it quickly became apparent that she controlled the family. Marie had successfully used the anger she had accumulated against her parents—the anger she felt because she believed her parents ignored her—by turning the anger into power over her parents.

During our interview we also found Marie had an appetite for MDMA—the designer drug "Ecstasy," which explained why she tested positive for amphetamines, because Ecstasy has an amphetamine base. Further questioning revealed Marie had been regularly sneaking out of her New Jersey neighborhood and traveling the hour or so to Manhattan, where she routinely attended rave parties.

The rave party scene in Manhattan consists of constant loud music, a lot of teen-age energy, sex, and drugs, starting around 11 P.M. or midnight in a warehouse or club. Mix in designer drugs, alcohol, and a revved-up scene that rolls until dawn, and you've got the rave scene down in a nutshell. Often, these are underground parties by invitation only. Many times there is a strong theme of love and understanding and acceptance of one another at these parties. In some ways they are a throw-back to the acid parties of the '60s without the bad acid trips. But unfortunately, there are other downsides to a rave.

Marie started in outpatient counseling but her urine tests continued to come back positive. We sent her to rehab, where she lasted only a few days. Because she did not show outward signs of withdrawal nor any other physical manifestations of chemical addiction she returned to us, where she continued outpatient counseling. Unfortunately, she still continued to use drugs—including occasionally dabbling in PCP. We tried to get the parents to become involved, but they continued to almost ignore their child.

We told the parents their daughter wasn't doing well, but the parents continued to minimize Marie's drug use. It became obvious that the parents, who had slipped into denial, had a healthy abuse and/or addiction problem themselves. We struggled to get them to admit this, if for no other reason than to help their daughter.

Meanwhile, Marie's drug use continued and, as she later told us, so did unprotected sex, which was at least occasionally on the menu at her favorite rave. Eventually she went for an HIV test and at the ripe old age of sixteen she tested positive for the AIDS virus.

Finally, her parents came around and said they would step in to stop Marie's slide and modify her behavior. We never saw Marie again.

The point is, of course, that parents need to become alert to all the underlying problems that can bring about a child's slide into abuse or addiction—and to act on what they find. This may mean a drastic modification of their own behavior, but further care for a child is pointless unless the parent sees and modifies his or her own self-destructive behavior.

"People in glass houses" may sound like a hoary old cliché, but it rings true, most especially to children.

Alert parents, besides engaging in self-analysis, must also analyze the family tree. Are there alcoholic cousins, aunts, uncles, parents, grandparents, brothers or sisters? Did close relatives ever have any other addiction or abuse problem? Genetics can play a large role in those who suffer from addiction. In that way it is very much like other disorders. A genetic tendency toward diabetes in your family may put you at greater risk of having diabetes yourself, but it is no guarantee you will eventually contract it. A history of addiction in your family may be an underlying cause of addiction in you or your children, but having addicts in your family tree does not guarantee you or your loved ones are condemned to addiction.

An alert parent will also take note of subtle behavioral abnormalities in their children. In many cases these activities may mean nothing when they are isolated occurrences. But a repetition of these behaviors should be looked at closely. Minor problems may not seem like much, but the parent should evaluate these minor problems if they occur in context with other minor or major problems.

Does your child bathe regularly? Good hygiene or bad hygiene may, unfortunately for the parents in some cases, merely be a statement of individuality; it could also be hiding an abuse and addiction habit. If the poor hygiene occurs in conjunction with other problems like tardiness or lethargy, the parent should see these events as warning signs. A child who usually exhibits good hygiene and then suddenly does not, should invite immediate scrutiny. Then again, a child who is obsessive about his or her appearance may be fine, but may also be trying to overcompensate for low self-esteem with cleanliness.

Look at your child's grades in school. Is a once-good student with excellent marks now doing poorly? Is your child not putting effort into his or her school work? Have you seen subtle signs of a personality change? Did your child used to be very punctual and now isn't? Does your child constantly switch friends?

A special area of behavior to look at that many parents can miss is the child's *fiscal responsibility.* A sudden need for money can be a warning sign of gambling addiction as well as alcohol or drug abuse.

Other areas of your child's behavior should be evaluated as well. They are not necessarily subtle changes, but they can be. An alert parent will assess each incident individually and with an eye on the overall picture of a child's personality.

PROBLEMS SLEEPING. If the child is not getting enough sleep, or sleeping too much, both can be symptoms of abuse or addiction. Children addicted to central nervous system (CNS) depressants, including alcohol, heroin, benzodiazepines, barbiturates, and even marijuana (which is not classified as a CNS depressant), are likely to sleep more than usual, while those addicted to cocaine or amphetamines, or who enjoy nibbling on LSD or Ecstasy will more than likely rarely rest and may make it difficult for a parent to sleep as well.

A child who wakes up in the middle of the night may be suffering from depression. *Bed wetting* at an older age can mean excessive drinking or other psychological problems. The particularly liquid display of bowel dysfunction popularized by the movie *Trainspotting* is also a consequence of heavy drug—particularly heroin—use.

In San Antonio, Texas, in the late 1980s, a local county sheriff's narcotics detective was able to identify the drug a suspected dealer was selling and abusing, and ultimately make a case because he noticed something strange about the suspect and his bed sheets.

While under surveillance on three separate occasions during the course of one week the suspect was seen purchasing the same size and color bed sheet at the same local Wal-Mart. The detective finally put it together and was later able to confirm his suspicions: the man was dealing and using heroin. Every two or three days, it seemed, he would soil his linens—under the influence of heroin. Rather than wash them, which took more work than the heroin high gave him the will to do, the lethargic heroin dealer merely ripped the sheets off the bed and stuffed them in his bedroom closet. Police estimated that nearly three months' worth of sheets (if he soiled them on average of once every three nights) were stuffed in the closet of the apartment he'd lived in for about three months. All of the sheets were the same powder blue. All of them were queen-sized, too, even though the dealer owned a twin bed. He told the county narcotics detectives during his interrogation that he didn't like to have tight-fitting sheets because it was more difficult to strip them from his soiled mattress.

Obviously an extreme case, but the point is, a teenager who soils his nightly linens should be closely scrutinized.

AN EXTREME PERSONALITY CHANGE "EVENT." The child who usually sits quietly at the dinner table and one day screams he can't eat tuna and noodles one more time may be a candidate for an "extreme" personality change, but is more likely a boisterous food critic. "Extreme" personality changes might include a *violent fight with a sibling*. If physical encounters between siblings are common in certain cases, we'd be looking at a marked increase in the severity of the physical encounter. *Kicking a family pet* can also be an example of a violent personality change. Repeated incidents of this should be looked at very seriously. Many times displaced anger can find an outlet in torturing pets and is a warning sign for possible abuse or addiction. *Fire setting* is an extreme sign of discomfort in the child and, unfortunately, a good sign of possible abuse or addiction. Any time a child becomes obsessed with starting fires, a parent should be concerned. Even if there is no abuse or addiction problem, other psychological problems are being manifested by this behavior.

IS THE CHILD STARTING TO HAVE MEMORY PROBLEMS? The short-term memory, as they say, is the first to go. If a child is not able to remember something from one minute to the next he may be as typical as a Cosby kid. Then again, a sudden loss of short-term memory could mean an addiction or abuse problem. A loss of short-term memory is also occasionally linked with *lethargic behavior*. This is especially true of those who are abusing CNS depressants or stimulants. Is your child slow getting up in the morning? Does he hate to get moving? He or she could be a typical adolescent, but this behavior in concert with other warning signs should be a tip-off that something is wrong, especially if the *child seems incoherent or listless*. All of these conditions, seen repeatedly together or separately, can mean a problem with abuse and addiction.

Suddenly quitting extracurricular activities, or rarely joining in those activities can both be signs of problems. The child who comes home and says he just grew bored with playing football after four years and wants to try something else may be telling you the truth, but may also be hiding a darker reason for quitting an activity; drug abuse or other forms of addiction may be taking over his life.

CRIMINAL BEHAVIOR. Is the child stealing? Is money missing from the home? Has your son or daughter been arrested or involved in an arrest?

Parents also need to look at *people, places, and things.* Are the kids hanging out near a known drug hangout? Do your children suddenly want to go out late at night? Parents need to be cognizant of evolving drug terminology. Many parents today have at least a passing familiarity with the drug culture from their own time as teenagers during the '60s and '70s. But today it pays to know the difference between a "blunt" and a "rock," or that a "dub" isn't a copy of a videotape. Be aware if a child begins to use strange terminology in and around the house.

As for *places,* a parent always needs to know where a child is going. Giving a child responsibility, latitude, and the freedom to make decisions about his or her life does not mean a parent gives up all involvement in the process. Also, even if the child says the parent is being excessively nosy, it doesn't necessarily mean the child is being truthful. It may be fashionable for a child to be upset with parents who always seem concerned, but on another level, the parent is telling the child that he or she cares. On that level the child appreciates the attention and needs it. *It cannot be overstated that an alert parent is one who is involved in his or her child's life even if the child says he doesn't want it.*

So find out where your children are spending their time. Ask questions. Does your child want to go to raves? Is your child often traveling to parties on farms miles outside of town? Is your child being allowed to go to parties where you don't know many of the participants? Are there entire blocks of time—hours or days—where you don't see or know what is going on with your child?

In addition to parental attention to the smallest detail, parents need to exercise *common sense*. If the child comes home acting drunk or stoned, the child probably is drunk or stoned. Amazingly, some parents, either unaware of the most obvious signs of inebriation or uncaring of them, never connect the dots.

Children will try to avoid appearing stoned or drunk, particularly if there is an abuse or addiction problem, but many times they take few precautions and many believe they can always fool the parent. Certainly most parents would know that, if their child comes home staggering and smelling like a brewery, then chances are the child is drunk. Most parents would probably also figure out that a child grinning like a Cheshire cat, smelling like burned rope, and with a bad case of the munchies is stoned on marijuana. Many parents would probably even figure out that if their child comes home and says the walls are breathing, he can catch his own hand, and has a propensity to believe Pink Floyd's "Wish You Were Here" is the greatest music ever made, he or she probably has a head filled with acid.

But most parents probably cannot distinguish between the manic movements of a crack and coke user, an amphetamine addict, or an obsessive-compulsive clean freak tripping on Ecstasy.

Parents should not only know the symptoms of the widely known drugs, but in certain environments should be aware of the symptoms of addiction to spray paint or other inhalants such as nitrous oxide, aerosols, glue, nitrates, or even white correction fluid ("wite-out").

These products produce certain physical symptoms, including nausea, headaches, lack of coordination, and atrophied motor skills, that parents should look for.

Parents should also be aware of strange and unidentifiable odors on a child's clothes or breath. A child who inhales spray paint (a "spray head") can sometimes end up with a face full of paint. Some upscale abusers of spray paint have successfully convinced their parents they were only building plastic models and had an accident with a can of spray paint. Children who have paint in their mouth or up their nose have a harder time selling that bit of fiction.

Watery, runny eyes and diarrhea may be symptoms of the flu, but in a teenager who comes home late, they may also be symptomatic of heroin abuse. Commonly abused drugs and their symptoms are shown in the chart on page 29.

Another popular drug for the adolescent set is "Special K" or ketamine. It is an animal tranquilizer and produces a state of numbness and a dreamlike state similar to Ecstasy or LSD. It also produces kids who are highly susceptible to suggestion in some cases, and has been known to be used as a "date rape" drug. It is usually snorted or taken orally but can be injected.

Meanwhile, if you suspect your son or daughter of a gambling problem, you should be on the lookout for money problems. Follow the money. Also, look for small pieces of paper with numbers written on them. If you see a slip of paper that says, for example, "Rams-7...times 5" it means your child's betting twenty-five bucks on the Rams game and giving the opponent seven points.

Gamblers can be excellent mathematicians, but even if your child isn't good with math he or she can have a betting problem. Be alert to see if your child begins avoiding telephone calls. Have you had strange people calling your child? It might be a sign of many problems, including your child being involved with a shylock. Gamblers also almost always have decks of cards around, as well as dice. Some tend to bet on the most obtuse things and this too can be a tipoff to the parent.

Finally, it cannot be stressed enough that an alert parent is not an over-reacting one. A boy who occasionally draws pictures of air-

Drug	Nickname or Street Name	Type	How Administered	Symptoms	Effects of Overdose	Withdrawal Symptoms
Ecstasy or MDMA,	X-stasy, Adam, XTC, essence, clarity	Hallucinogenic	Pill or capsule	Hyperactivity, seizures, altered mood, perception changes similar to LSD	Similar to LSD	None reported
LSD	acid, orange sunshine, Microdot, Window Pane, Purple Haze	Hallucinogenic	Odorless, colorless, tasteless. Can be in liquid form, like eye-drops, or in tablets, blotter paper, candy ("Window Pane")	Emotional instability, possible violent activity, excessive laugh-ter, vivid hallucinations, trance-like focus, dilated pupils, sweating, loss of appetite, tremors	Psychosis, deeper "trips"	None reported
Marijuana and hashish	Pot, dope, grass, weed, smoke	Central nervous system stimulant	Smoked in a pipe or in cigarette form; eaten in baked products (e.g., cookies, brownies)	Distorted perception, confusion of senses, anxiety, "cotton mouth," "laughter, panic attacks, "munchies"	Lethargy, sleepiness, fatigue, paranoia	Insomnia, hyperac-tivity; otherwise, no physical signs of withdrawal
Heroin	H, horse	Narcotic, central nervous system depressant	Injected, snorted, taken orally injected, snorted, smoked	A "rush," euphoria, drowsiness, dry mouth, high body tempera-ture, nausea, constricted pupils	Slow, shallow breathing, clammy skin, convulsions, irritability, tremors,panic	Watery eyes, runny nose, yawning, no appetite, chills, cramps, nausea
Cocaine or crack	Snow, blow, toot, C, rock	Stimulant	Snorted, smoked, injected	Increased alertness, excitation, euphoria, increased pulse rate, increased blood pressure, loss of appetite, hyperactivity, excessive energy, paranoia	Agitation, increase in body temperature, convulsions, looking "flushed"	Apathy, long periods of sleep, irritability, depression
Speed	Uppers, Black Beauties, Christmas Trees	Stimulant	Same as cocaine	Same as cocaine	Similar to cocaine	Similar to cocaine

planes shooting at each other is not necessarily a boy who will become an addict or enter his school armed with shotguns and bombs. Many behaviors that are warning signs of addiction can also show up in teens who are quite healthy. It is the recurrence of some of these behaviors combined with their clustering that will lead an alert parent to focus additional attention on the child.

The alarm has to sound *if the behavior is becoming obsessive.*

Some other behavior that alert parents need to recognize includes, but is not limited to, the following:

■ Taking wild chances. Thrill-seeking and extreme sports can be a lot of fun, and certainly a child who loves to emulate Tony Hawke on a skate board isn't necessarily a child to become worried about, but sometimes taking wild chances is a mask for low self-esteem.

■ Acting like Rambo or a bully. A bully is often the easiest child in the world to become angry with. But every bully, at his or her heart, is a child scarred by low self-esteem.

■ The fawning pleaser. These are kids who go out of their way to please others—some even to the point where they will steal money from their parents in order to treat their friends just so their friends won't leave them and abandon them.

■ "I can't decide." The child who has problems making even the simplest decisions—such as what to wear, what to eat, how to act—is usually a child with a low self-esteem.

■ Self-mutilation. Puncture wounds, cuttings, compulsive hair-pulling, and other self-destructive physical actions are signs of very deep emotional trauma.

What is surprising is that disorders previously not regarded as addictive illnesses in fact are. Co-dependence and even compulsive shopping are included in the addiction category and can be success-fully treated with therapeutic techniques developed to treat physical addictions. Recent clinical observations support a unified theory of addictive illnesses as variations of one disorder with a common underlying feature: low self-esteem. The elements of low self-esteem include recurring feelings of insecurity, inadequacy, and inferiority. People who suffer from any form of addictive illness entertain more of this negative thinking and poor self-image than the rest of the population.

Obviously, parents need to spend a lot of time with children to teach them to act responsibly. You may not be able to teach a child not to drink, but perhaps you can teach your child not to drink and drive. Spend the time to influence your children.

If an alert parent is a caring parent and the home has a healthy atmosphere, the chances of abuse and addiction are smaller. Set limits, discipline your child—but never in anger. It's okay to be angry, but be careful how you direct your anger to your children. It is okay to let a child know you are angry, but never act from that anger. Striking a child and telling him you're upset, or screaming and yelling at him with obscenities isn't as effective as calmly letting a child know that you, the parent, are angry and that the child's behavior has to be modified. Following these simple guidelines can help keep your child from bouts of low self-esteem, and the chances are you'll keep your child from abuse and addiction.

CHAPTER 2
Before addiction, low self-esteem

I'm pretty sure my child isn't into drugs,
but he's always depressed.

IT STARTS AT AN EARLY AGE. It is hard to imagine anything more completely helpless-looking than a child suffering from depression or low self-esteem. Coaches see it in youth sports at a very early age. It is the child who throws the bat down and won't play. It is the child who cries when you put him or her in the game, or the child who cannot play as well as his peers and throw tantrums or sulks because of it. At ages as early as five and six, children will exhibit these behaviors.

These children lack confidence in themselves and often feel bad about it or act out of fear because of their lack of confidence. "I'm no good. I stink. Everybody else is better than me," is the hallmark of a child who feels inadequate about him or herself. Other children and even adults can then play on that insecurity, creating a feedback loop that leads to low self-esteem.

Parents can also exacerbate the problem. A child who cries at a soccer game or Little League baseball game and is greeted by a screaming or yelling parent isn't likely to feel good about himself any time soon. Yet it isn't uncommon to see parents on the sports fields yelling at their own children, the opposition, the coaches, or even each other. A recent encounter in California led to several arrests of parents after one adult struck another with a metal rod during a soccer match.

In some cases the problems of parents out of control have led to extreme measures. For example, the Recreation Department in

Montgomery County, Maryland, makes all parents who sign their children up for basketball also sign an agreement and return it to the county pledging that they will act like adults and limit their antics during the course of the game—or suffer automatic ejection.

Imagine the fear and confusion in a young child who sees his or her parents acting out in a violent manner, and then combine that fear with the peer pressure and self-loathing that an unconfident child feels, and you may begin to understand the seeds of low self-esteem. The combination of peer and parental pressure can lead to a host of problems in children, and as we previously highlighted, depression can be an indication of low self-esteem, abuse, and/or addiction. These children never or rarely feel good about themselves.

Often, while counseling substance abusers and addicts, we have asked, "*Why do you get high?*" We always hear the same answer: "*I get high to feel good.*"

Logically, we then ask the following series of questions: "*Can you remember how you felt the last time you were drug free? Did you feel good about yourself? Did you like being you? Were you happy?*" The answer from ninety-nine out of a hundred addicts was an astounding "*No!*" to every question.

After we record those answers we then ask this series of questions: "*Do you feel other kids are better than you? Are you afraid to talk to people for fear of saying something wrong or stupid? Do you feel that money, success, or power will help you to be liked and loved by others? Do your parents make you feel inadequate?*"

These questions help determine whether a child is having a self-esteem problem. Healthy self-esteem, marked by self-confidence and comfort with oneself, is sorely lacking in children with abuse and addiction problems. Children with low self-esteem are those who often say, "I can't." They may actually feel more comfortable in failure than in success because of the familiarity of failure. These children wear their failure like a worn overcoat. It is familiar and comfortable, and although it may not feed their low self-esteem and, like a worn overcoat, will not protect them from the elements, at least the failure is familiar. It is hard to break that cycle of low self-esteem and depression.

Generally, people with low self-esteem immerse themselves in self-destructive behavior. Substance abuse and other addictive illnesses represent the antithesis of self-care and healthy self-esteem. But before addiction takes hold, a common array of emotional dynamics occurs, usually during the addict's childhood. Feelings of insecurity make us feel like we can't do things that other people can, that we aren't able to accomplish what we might like. The symptoms of low self-esteem include aspects of guilt, shame, anger, fear, perfectionism, and stress. These emotions make us feel less than whole and can be quite upsetting, causing distress. Chemicals like alcohol and other drugs come into play here because they create a soothing effect that tranquilizes the feelings of insecurity. They provide a temporary escape, hence the term "self-medicating." The abuser or addict is not getting high or drunk for the sake of the high, but to dull the feelings of low self-esteem he or she feels constantly. Compulsive shoppers and gamblers get the same type of high, and studies have even shown that the same centers of the brain are stimulated by gambling as by cocaine.

IN MANY CASES, CHILDREN WILL GIVE YOU A TIP-OFF to their lack of self-esteem by displaying some of the symptoms we discussed in Chapter 1. Other times they may not, and an alert parent has to look for the clues.

The first thing a parent has to look for outside the home is that all-important *peer pressure.*

It cannot be overstated how important "fitting in" is to an adolescent, and it doesn't necessarily have to be "fitting in" with "the right crowd." Many times the adolescent coming straight out of childhood still idolizes his or her parents, but is beginning to become aware of the larger world around him. There is, thus, also a need to pull away from the parent and seek others like themselves. How many of us were so wise at the age of twelve or thirteen that we didn't make some fundamental errors in our judgment about that larger world and our parents?

That is the problem young teens face as they look for peers to accept them, nurture them, and offer them friendship. Peer pressure, therefore, is one of the biggest factors in self-esteem for an adolescent, and since there are so many types of peer pressure, we've broken them up to examine them more thoroughly.

SEXUAL PEER PRESSURE. Boys traditionally have been the aggressors in this area, but today's teens may just as likely see girls in this role. The pressure is applied by those pursuing and those being pursued. The media help because television shows and advertising flaunt sexuality. Children come to believe that having sex is vital to their life, and children with low self-esteem will not only buy into this idea, but might end up doing anything to please a mate, as long as they feel there is some kind of relationship. But, as we all know, some teens will take advantage of this and use someone for sexual experimentation and nothing else. Children with low self-esteem will think even less of themselves as they come to realize they've been used in such a manner.

In fact, a lot of women we see in the drug culture started off in their adolescence badly needing male companionship. This need for male nurturing lured them into the drug culture. They finally found a boy or a guy who would spend time with them but who unfortunately was also a drug addict. The girls in these cases began using drugs not so much to get high, but to have something in common with their boyfriends.

The lure to share is very strong in human beings, as is the need to find common ground, and it often goes beyond logic. Those suffering from low self-esteem feel their boyfriend or girlfriend will not leave them while immersed in drugs, so they have a common bond. But after extended use the drugs take on a life of their own, and by then you have someone who not only needs male or female nurturing, but is also a drug addict. That's how the relationship continues until one of them hits bottom either physically or mentally. That's usually when we enter the picture and try to make the patient understand that it was low self-esteem that brought him or her to our doorstep.

No person who thinks highly of himself would be lured into drugs for the sake of a relationship with another human being. However, people who have a history of abuse or neglect often fall into this trap.

NONSEXUAL PEER PRESSURE. Another of the biggest stressors a child can have is nonsexual peer pressure. It can come from such things as inadequate food, clothing, and shelter. Or other children may pick on a child because of poor hygiene. Learning disabilities or being inadequate at sports or scholastically can also add stress, which can lead to abuse or addiction. We once had a child who was very upset about being on the "little yellow bus" going to school instead of the larger bus because other kids referred to the smaller bus as "the retard bus." This led the child down a very destructive path.

Color can definitely be part of the equation. Kids can be cruel, and children of mixed races can suffer from peer pressure. They can have problems because their father is black and their mother is white, or some variation. Various speech impediments, common enough in smaller children and usually something they grow out of, can also influence peer pressure. Overweight kids can face particularly cruel teasing.

As most adults have come to realize, all types of peer pressure are normal aspects of growing up. There is much talk of bullies and peer pressure in our children's lives because of incidents such as the attack in Columbine High School in Littleton, Colorado, but these pressures have been around for a very long time. We have all faced the inevitable comparison and evaluations of our peers. It has escalated because parents today are not adequately engaged in their children's life. School systems cannot raise a child alone, and yet in many cases parents have ceded part or all of their parental responsibility to the school system. The child with low self-esteem whose parents are not involved has turned peer pressure into something potentially dangerous.

LACK OF ATTENTION. A child who gets no attention from his or her parents or has few friends feels left out, alone, and often frightened. As we've already said, this alone can cause monumental problems.

SPIRITUAL NEGLECT. Children who have unanswered questions regarding their spirituality and feel no one is filling that void can also suffer from low self-esteem. Alcoholics Anonymous and Narcotics Anonymous are effective because they treat the need for spiritual sustenance. How parents address the needs of the spirit is, of course, up to the individual parent. But it cannot be overstated how much a parent needs at least to *address* the issue. We all have questions of why we are here and what our role is in the universe. A parent who ignores or refuses to address this very important topic does so at the risk of putting his child in peril.

PHYSICAL ATTRIBUTES. Low self-esteem can be brought on merely by the size of a child's nose, or an exceptionally harsh case of acne. But more importantly, a parent who doesn't deal with these issues can also lead the child into low self-esteem.

Many times all of the factors we've mentioned, or a combination of them, will lead to the problems of low self-esteem. This brings to mind a case of a sixteen-year-old girl named Jeannie. She was short in stature and had not developed secondary sexual characteristics, making her feel uncomfortable. Watching television, looking at boys who seemed to get excited over ample cleavage, and viewing herself as unattractive led her into a spiral of depression.

Her mother was the only caregiver at the time—her father did not live at home. The mother was very conscious of her daughter's weight and looks and was concerned about her. The girl came into therapy and became convinced that she needed to have her breasts enlarged in order to feel better about herself. Her mother agreed, and both reasoned that with an operation Jeannie would start to feel good about herself because she would get more attention from her peers—especially boys.

Against our advice and after cautioning both Jeannie and her mother that more therapy was needed, Jeannie had breast implants. Consequently, the young teen had a more robust cleavage and began to get hit on by more guys. But they were only interested in sex, and Jeannie continued her spiral into low self-esteem and depression. At that point Jeannie's mother got her back into therapy because she didn't know what was really bothering her daughter.

As it turned out the real issue was not about the way Jeannie looked, but about her estranged father. Since her father wasn't around she was starved for any male attention and became convinced she wasn't getting it because of the way she looked. The implants didn't help her self-esteem, but rather fueled the fire because the resulting male attention was not what she was looking for.

By the time she was seventeen and had been in therapy for several more months she came to realize that she was trying to get her self-esteem from her peers and not from herself.

KIDS IN A SEXUAL CRISIS. Many children questioning their own sexuality get their mothers "in a whirl" and their fathers too when the parents don't know if their child is exhibiting behaviors of a boy or a girl. These children are potentially the most dangerous to themselves. A child in a sexual crisis is not only a child with potential self-esteem problems. In bouts of depression these children have been known to take their own life.

Another case comes to mind, and we'll call him Eddie. Eddie realized he was homosexual at an early age, decided to come out of the closet, and started to wear "flamer" clothing. He appeared to accept himself. But as soon as he began dressing flamboyantly other children reacted. He got beat up in school and he was made fun of. This threw Eddie into a spiral of depression. As is often the case, it was someone outside of himself who lowered his self-esteem. He began abusing marijuana and eventually got into cocaine, heroin, and Ecstasy. Eddie got into a situation where he didn't even want to go to school anymore because of his homosexuality.

Finally, his despair and deep depression led to a couple of suicide attempts.

In therapy Eddie talked about the demeaning things other children had done to him and how he was beaten up quite a bit. He came to believe he needed a fresh start, and that there were other people around him who were not sexually in touch with themselves or comfortable with their own sexuality. Further, Eddie came to see that his manner of dress was an attempt to get acceptance from his peers. If he was enlightened, then so should the rest of the world be. When he was greeted with indifference and anger he lost his confidence and self-esteem.

Eddie came to believe that he was going over the top with his manner of dress needlessly. He decided to dress comfortably, but sensibly, and then began to deal with his feelings of inadequacy, inferiority, and insecurity. His parents also decided to give him a fresh start at a new school so Eddie could attend classes without living in fear of getting beaten up.

Finally, after Eddie and his parents came to these different conclusions, he was able to get off the antidepressants that had helped him with his depression and had also helped him stay away from other drugs. Eddie also sought out a gay AA meeting where he could find others who would accept him. Eddie went on to do very well for himself.

BEING THE NEW KID IN TOWN. While Eddie made a calculated move to a new school, many times a change of scenery can be a stressful situation for an adolescent.

Delab was an Indian boy who came to us for treatment because of a substance abuse problem. He was fluent in English, but had a very marked accent. He was very bright, but not well coordinated and wasn't involved much in sports. He had trouble making friends in a new school environment and ended up making friends with the least discriminating group of kids among his peers—the burnouts and druggies. He found validation and acceptance among this group but was eventually caught by a urine test at school. His parents had no idea he had a problem with drugs.

In therapy it came out that what was fueling his low self-esteem was the feeling that he wasn't as good as other kids because of his language barrier, his lack of interest in sports, and his feeling that he couldn't fit in or conform. After several months of therapy Delab began to change his opinion of himself and came to like himself more and came to realize he deserved love, value, and respect as a human being. He stopped using drugs and began to focus more on his own opinion of his self-worth.

PHYSICAL OR EMOTIONAL TRAUMA. Night terrors, nightmares, the inability to sleep, throwing oneself out of bed are all symptomatic of trauma. A child who has had physical or emotional trauma has suffered a stressful experience that can destroy self-esteem.

This can be over something as benign-sounding as a sports injury. A child who has been an athlete and excelled at sports most of his life and suddenly finds that his sports career is in question because of a major injury can lose a lot of self-esteem and go straight into depression.

Also, children of newly divorced parents or children who are in an environment where they are constantly being yelled at or demeaned by a parent or guardian usually have major problems with their self-esteem.

OBSESSIVE-COMPULSIVE DISORDERS. Sometimes this situation can be corrected by the proper medication. A good psychiatrist can provide a medical evaluation to determine this. Jack Nicholson's character in the movie *As Good As It Gets* is a classic example of someone with an obsessive-compulsive disorder. He had to count the number of times he closed and locked his door. It had to be done in the same way every time. He washed his hands each time with a fresh bar of soap. He wouldn't walk on cracks in the sidewalk and he drove people nuts at the one restaurant he would frequent.

Many of these disorders can now be successfully treated with some form of medication, even if the patient hates taking pills, like Nicholson's character did. However, sometimes obsessive-compulsive disorders cannot be successfully treated with medication alone. Sometimes it takes a combination of therapy and medication, or perhaps only therapy. In some cases obsessive-compulsive behavior may be a symptom of low self-esteem that can only be treated when the patient is aware of the underlying cause of the low self-esteem.

Obsessive-compulsive disorders can be viewed as a protective shield—a built-in self-defense mechanism to deal with underlying issues that haven't been dealt with consciously. What we try to do is to find out why the person is obsessively doing what he or she is doing because if we expose the hidden cause of the behavior then usually we can help the client get that behavior to stop.

Donna was a patient of ours who started to drink quite frequently, and she came to us from a psychiatrist who diagnosed her as having an obsessive-compulsive disorder. She had been on various medications for this disorder for a long time, but she felt she wasn't getting anything from them and she began to self-medicate with alcohol.

That's when she came to see us. Donna was a "clean freak" whose house had to be spotless at all times. She was constantly cleaning, washing, and scrubbing to the point of wearing the skin off her hands. Her obsessive behavior affected her children, whom she always had to have dressed up as neat as a pin. Everything had to be perfect in Donna's world.

After having Donna in therapy for a while we identified the underlying cause of her obsessive-compulsive behavior as a problem she had with her mother and father as a little girl. Donna's mother had been a perfectionist and put a very strong emphasis on cleanliness. Meanwhile, her father, an alcoholic, was out of the picture. Donna's mother, in an effort to control the situation, had Donna clean the house. If the house was clean she wouldn't get any kudos from her mother, but if there was one spot of dirt, Donna would suffer verbal and at times physical abuse from her mother. Donna carried feelings of inadequacy and inferiority caused by this trauma into adulthood. After a time in treatment, she realized that her current behavior stemmed from events that had occurred nearly thirty years previously. The obsessive-compulsive activity had been taught to her by her mother, and Donna had used that behavior to hide from her continuing feelings of inadequacy and inferiority.

Donna finally became aware of why she was a compulsive "clean freak." She believed that immaculate living conditions gave her total control. In turn, she was putting pressure on her own children. She finally knew why she was hitting the bottle and eventually gave it up. Donna came to realize she wasn't a failure and she didn't need to continue to try to be perfect by being perfectly clean.

Donna's case is also indicative of *parental programming*, which often can lead to low self-esteem. From the time we are very small and become aware of our surroundings, we are aware that we need to be fed, clothed, and taken care of. Parents usually fill that bill nicely and it isn't odd for us to put our parents up on pedestals as gods. We then experience their moods, their happiness, their sadness, and all the other experiences of their lives. We can become the product of our parenting. By our parents' actions and inactions, conscious and unconscious, we learn what is acceptable behavior and what is important, and we learn who we are and what type of people we are. That is how our parents program us.

That's why some of the hardest cases for us involve *physical and sexual abuse* in the family. Particularly in physically abusive situations, the children create a guilt cycle that justifies and anticipates the physical violence their parents will visit upon them. "I feel guilty" is the emotion the child begins with. That progresses to "I feel guilty so I've done something bad," which in turn progresses to "I deserve to be punished." Such a child, trapped in this mind-set, will act out his or her self-destructive behavior in a kind of self-fulfilling prophecy that will actually encourage parental physical abuse. The child, who has put his or her parents on a pedestal, personalizes the abuse he receives, reasoning that "If I wasn't bad, Daddy or Mommy wouldn't have punished me so severely." The same rationalization is used by children who are sexually abused. These children actually come to believe that it is their behavior that has induced one or both of their parents to sexually abuse them. You can imagine what this does to someone's self-esteem. It crushes it. Many times children like this come into therapy telling us they deserved exactly what they got.

This belief induces shame in the child, and shame, a very powerful feeling, causes anxiety, depression, and angst along with the destruction of self-esteem. Many times these children try to alleviate their negative, uncomfortable feelings with alcohol and other drugs or some other form of addiction and abuse. These children come to think that not only do they deserve what has happened to them, but in some intangible way they are defective.

So, as we can see, there are many causes of low self-esteem. It can be something as simple as wearing braces, and something as hideous as sexual abuse. But the bottom line for all of those who suffer from low self-esteem is that they feel incomplete or broken.

Many times this can lead down the garden path to self-destructive abuse or addiction. But, before they get there, often there is another factor, a traveling companion with low self-esteem: Anger.

CHAPTER 3
Unresolved anger

My child doesn't appear angry, but is often sullen.
Am I missing something?

RECENTLY TWO CHILDREN IN A SUBURBAN MARYLAND MIDDLE SCHOOL
got into a fistfight typical of sixth graders. One boy, egged on by his
friends, had been picking on another boy for about two weeks. Each
day as the second child sat down in the lunchroom, the first child
approached him and told him he couldn't sit where he wanted to.

The second boy had been told by his parents to try to talk his way
out of any problem and, although he was angry with the other child
for picking on him, he tried to talk his way out of the situation. The
first child concluded the second child was a pushover and he shoved
him. The second child responded by standing up and hitting the first
child several times until the fight was broken up by an administrator.

Clearly there was anger involved in the altercation. The second
child, angry at being picked on, lashed out when struck by another
child. The second child allowed anger to build, or indeed created a
dam to contain his anger until he unleashed it. Anger is natural and
anger can be used effectively, but the danger in creating a dam
behind which you try to contain your anger can be self-defeating.

For example, what anger motivated the first child to pick on the
second? As it turned out the child had a number of problems stem-
ming from a broken home and the fact that both of his parents had
remarried. He consequently suffered from a lack of male nurturing
from his specific-gender parent, his father. This made him angry and
he didn't know how to deal with that anger. One way the boy dealt
with it was to seek the company of other young males as a substitute

for the lack of nurturing from his father. But the boy became more angry and was also easily manipulated by these new friends. He was attempting to find an outlet for his own emotions, including anger, by picking on another child.

The anger dam had caused an unhealthy diversion in the river of the first boy's emotions. Anger must be allowed to flow freely, but channeled in healthy directions.

Misdirected anger can be a potent force, and particularly debilitating when turned inward toward one's self. Children can learn to be afraid of anger when they experience it in connection with punishment or abuse, often received from their parents. They can wind up believing that anger literally hurts others. That misperception can have a powerful allure too if the child comes to believe that literally hurting others is preferable. Violence addicts and school shootings attest to some of the worst-case scenarios in this regard.

But also possible, and equally if not more probable, is that the child will turn his or her anger inward, trying to hide it and prevent it from escaping. Internalized anger is emotionally toxic; it can cause depression and prevent people from ever developing a healthy self-esteem. At worst, suicidal tendencies can be seen in those who internalize their anger.

Adults who are co-dependent tend to focus on their own anger, but are also scared of anger in others. Seeing a loved one angry sets up anxiety or fear for the relationship. To avoid anger, co-dependents will often compromise themselves in any way required to ensure they won't make anyone around them angry. They're afraid that if someone they care about gets mad, that person will be alienated and start to move away, just as they worry that if they display their own anger, they will alienate a loved one.

We categorize internalized anger as an unresolved conflict within the person. In a child it sets them up for depression because children may not have the tools of experience needed to handle their anger. They are resentful. In his book *Feeling Good,* Dr. David Burns categorizes the Four D's that lead to low self-esteem or depression: **Deserted, Defeated, Defective, or Deprived.** We use these guidelines in our practice to keep tabs on our patients' anger.

The Four D's. When people have a lot of unresolved anger, they feel defeated. They feel they cannot successfully express their feelings. They may feel deprived of a safe place to be angry. And if they feel they have no safe place to express their feelings, they can feel deserted. Those who feel this way can come to believe there is something wrong with them. If they were good people, or effective people, so they reason, then they could solve their problem. Eventually those with low self-esteem will come to believe they are the problem. They think they are wrong. They think they are defective.

In the previous example of two children fighting in middle school, the first child had expressed feelings of being deserted, defective, defeated, and deprived on occasion to parents, teachers, and administrators, not only in words, but in deeds. At the beginning of the school year this child was sent home early from an outdoor education course because he had tripped another child and done bodily injury to another child. The child readily confessed each transgression and eagerly promised to change.

But the boy's unresolved conflict with his father was at the core of the problem. Every time he got into trouble, his father arrived. It was the boy's desperate attempts to bring his father into his life, fueled by low self-esteem, which caused the anger, which enhanced the low self-esteem, which brought about the fight, which got him a suspension, and which caused the parents to shake their heads and ask, "Why?"

But much like the House That Jack Built, the parents knew why, if only they could follow the chain of events.

Children sometimes fail to turn their feelings into language, thereby dealing with their unresolved conflict. Parents can cause problems by being the source of the child's anger. Children often idolize their parents, sometimes even when the parent does not warrant anything close to respect, never mind adulation. Children therefore will be less likely to voice anger against their parents. Later on we'll discuss how parents can allow children to voice their anger at them in a healthy manner, but suffice it to say here that it must be done. Parents who deny their children the ability to voice their anger at them are setting themselves and their children up for a potentially nasty fall.

Remember: Anger is a river. As long as the river flows, it is fine. Children must feel safe in expressing thoughts and feelings, especially of anger—even if the child is angry at his or her own parent.

Parents must encourage children to turn thoughts and feelings into language, to speak about them and thereby get rid of them. Kicking pets, starting fires, acting out, starting fights—these are all indications that a child has anger issues. The child is not finding a healthy outlet for his or her anger, the anger is building behind a dam and it is seeping out in various ways.

A child who is finding an unhealthy outlet for his anger may even begin to fantasize about violence. It is no coincidence that many of the perpetrators of recent school violence reportedly fantasized about doing something violent before it actually became a hideous and bloody reality. That too is a warning sign. Other children are often in the best position to see this type of warning sign, but are often not coached in the correct manner to bring it to the attention of an adult.

Children, if taught at all to inform school administrators about violence, are often told to do so immediately. In the example of the two boys fighting in middle school, the child who had been picked on was urged to stand up immediately, whether in class or the public lunch room, and let an adult know he was being picked on. Unfortunately, in the world of a child, there is no greater target than a "snitch," and no sixth grader with any common sense is going to incur the wrath of his or her peers by publicly ratting on someone else.

But the information many children possess could deter potential fatal violence by their peers. Children too need to be aware of the warning signs of low self-esteem and depression and thus ward off potential violence, but school administrators must learn to coach children *how* to inform them.

Anger can also be seen in passivity—not eating, not finishing homework, being lazy, and a variety of other behaviors. Many times kids will start to screw up in school just to get back at their parents. They may start to move into the drug culture too as a way of paying back their parents since they are unable to unload anger and emotion in a healthy way at home.

Several psychosomatic conditions can arise from anger. Some of them connected with internalized anger are colitis, ileitis, hypertension, intense headaches, ulcers, immune system depression, asthma attacks, and certainly heart disease. One of the biggest factors in heart attacks is anger.

Never forget how toxic internalized anger can be.

The capacity to feel anger is natural. Many believe fear and hurt are underneath the anger, and that is certainly an appropriate observation. In any case, anger is a clear signal something is wrong and something that others can see. Those with the best chance of defusing the anger of children are parents, if they are involved in their child's life.

Children who are being abused, verbally or physically, and never get to resolve the problem will feel they are "all alone" or deserted and separated from everyone else. They don't have a chance to express their feelings adequately and may feel they don't have a safe place to do so. Inevitably, such children begin to feel there is something wrong with them.

"If I was okay, then Mommy or Daddy wouldn't treat me this way," may go the reasoning. This is often seen in children of divorced parents, who believe that they are responsible in some way for the divorce. "Mommy and Daddy would've stayed together if it wasn't for me," they will say. Such feelings are expressions of children who feel they are defective. So, one can see that unresolved conflict and emotional problems in children can lead to these four D's, a result of internalized anger.

What the child is really trying to come to grips with, and often fails to do because of a lack of worldly experience, is that he is *angry*. The child is angry at being abused, or the child is angry with his parents for divorcing, or any of a number of other things. But because children look up to parents and often have the idea that parents are "all knowing," the child cannot understand his anger and ultimately blames himself for the anger.

We have often said, in treating children, anger is like a river, and as long as the river is flowing things are fine. Dam up the river of anger and what you risk is trouble. The dam ultimately, and always, will break. Unfortunately in doing so a child may suffer more than if the anger were allowed to work itself out in a more natural fashion.

It cannot be understated:

CHILDREN MUST BE ABLE TO EXPRESS THEIR FEELINGS

Anger is a powerful feeling, a potentially explosive emotion that must be dealt with by a parent. Urging a child to "buck up" and go on, or to "put it away" isn't a healthy way to deal with anger. Urge the child to express his anger before you urge the child to "buck up." Children must feel safe in expressing their anger. If they do not, if they may not express their anger in front of a parent, they will find ways to express it, influenced by the "Four D's," that will not be healthy.

Take William, for example. William was in kindergarten and got the reputation for being a bully. This shocked his mother, who always found her son to be sweet and sometimes even obsequious at home. But William's mother came to find that her son was harboring extreme anger and resentment.

The cause was William's father. His father had never married his mother—he had signed away parental rights and didn't seem to be interested in his son. William knew he must have a father and later called the man his mother eventually married, "Father."

But he still wanted to know about his "real dad." His mother, however, felt for a variety of reasons that since the father didn't want to do anything for his son, he could have no contact with the boy, and the boy didn't need to waste his time on an uncaring and unsupportive father. At an early age the child became angry and didn't know what to do with his anger. He lashed out at school and had increasing trouble there. By the sixth grade he was in therapy, where it came to light that he was angry with his "real father" for deserting him, and at his mother, who he believed had helped keep him from his birth father.

That's why therapy is extremely important in dealing with anger. When you talk about your feelings you can begin to understand the causes of your anger. Many times you may not be fully aware why you are angry until you begin to talk about it. Talking about it, and working it out, keep the anger river flowing. Turning your anger into language and getting rid of it in such a manner is extremely helpful and healthy.

Otherwise, as in William's case, the anger will work itself out in unhealthy ways, like being a bully. You can also see this anger in children who hurt the family pet, or start fires, or are extremely passive and don't complete their school work, or don't eat. Anorexic children may be trying to get back at their parents by hurting themselves by not eating and losing weight. Obsessive-compulsive disorders can be indicative of this internalized anger, and so can passive-aggressive behavior.

Sometimes children who have a track record of exemplary school work will begin to ditch the work and ruin their grades in order to get back at parents with whom they are angry. It is important to note that this may not be a parent who is abusing or otherwise inflicting great harm on a child.

The parent can be an exemplary parent, but it is the child's *per-ception* of what the parent is doing to him or her that leads to the internalized anger, low self-esteem, and eventually self-destructive behavior. It has often been said that you never truly understand someone until you walk a mile in his shoes. The saying may well have been written by a parent struggling to understand her child. Many times things that occur to children may not seem like much, particularly to a parent who perhaps experienced something similar as a child and lived through it without adverse consequences, or perhaps faced a similar challenge later in life and did not suffer unduly. However, it is important to understand how the *individual child* is uniquely experiencing the rejection or the setback.

Take a look at a child who plays youth soccer. He or she runs out to kick the ball, misses, and the opposing team takes the ball and scores. It may not even be the winning score, but the child was scored upon. To everyone else, every spectator, every child, the coach, and the parents, the missed kick is part of the game or at the very worst, a mistake that anyone can make and something not worth worrying about. But to the child who missed the kick, and if it is reinforced by other similar mistakes, the action can have catastrophic results. Which isn't to say that a child of eight or nine who misses a kick on the soccer field, or drops a fly ball in the outfield, or misses an open field tackle will end up being a drug abuser or addict, but the activities of such a child do mean more to the child and may seem more catastrophic to that child than to anyone else in the world. A parent must recognize that and deal with it before a child begins to internalize the anger he or she feels about the behavior.

Jimmy came to us when he was sixteen years old. His mother brought him in saying that Jimmy was acting out with a lot of defiance and she thought Jimmy might be using drugs. We asked, as we normally do, to see her and Jimmy's father, but she explained that the father was working and couldn't be counted on to attend therapy.

Further, the mother said that Jimmy was staying out late at night, was stealing the family car when he wanted to get out, and had gotten into some fights. Basically, she said her child was very "angry" and was becoming abusive. We took a urine sample from Jimmy and it came back positive for cocaine. At that point we insisted on beginning counseling with the whole family. But the father always had an excuse for not showing up.

Meanwhile, Jimmy continued his slide into drug abuse and addiction. He met a Colombian drug dealer and decided at some point he was going to kill the dealer, steal his stash of drugs, then just take an overdose and die. When we found out in a therapy session what he had in mind we sent Jimmy to a rehab, where he stayed for twenty-eight days until he returned to us.

By then we desperately wanted to get the father into the family sessions, but the father still refused. The mother continued to make excuses for him, but we finally called her on the carpet to try and find out what was wrong. It already appeared that Jimmy had a lot of unresolved and internalized anger toward his father. Jimmy was under the impression his father didn't care about him, and by not showing up at the therapy sessions, the father was only reinforcing those feelings. Jimmy also told us that his father had gone out of his way to put Jimmy down in front of his mother and was very demeaning whenever he spoke to him.

The mother just shrugged when we confronted her and we were still unsuccessful at getting the father into the family therapy sessions. Then the situation got worse. While Jimmy continued to come to outpatient treatment and began to go to Alcoholics Anonymous meetings, he also continued to use drugs. By now he was not only snorting cocaine, but shooting it up and, worse, shooting up heroin as well. Sometimes, like the late comedian John Belushi, Jimmy was "speedballing"—shooting up a combination of cocaine and heroin.

When we became aware of this it was obviously a medical necessity to get Jimmy back into rehab and medically stabilized before he died. But he didn't get any better and continued to use drugs, finally becoming jaundiced and contracting hepatitis B. He was also arrested and charged with drug possession. With that development we were able to use the court system to force the father into therapy sessions with his son, and that's when it all came to a head.

Our first step was to evaluate the father, and, unsurprisingly, we found out that he didn't have a very good relationship with his wife and his son. He had married Jimmy's mother because she fulfilled a need for a mother figure in his life. After Jimmy was born, the father became jealous of the attention his wife gave to his son and began to have a sort of sibling rivalry with his own son.

It was a very unhealthy situation that led to several rage-filled sessions in which the father and the son confronted these unspoken and internalized feelings toward each other. Several sessions were filled with yelling and screaming between the two as Jimmy accused his father of not loving and not caring about him. Finally, the anger began to subside and the sessions became more introspective and less rancorous.

What had happened was that Jimmy was allowed to take all of the toxic, negative, and angry feelings he had kept inside for many years and turn them into words that he spewed at his father. Jimmy stopped doing drugs as he became aware that he didn't have to self-medicate to hide from those uncomfortable thoughts and feelings.

Life also improved for the father as he realized his wife was not his mother and that Jimmy was not a sibling, but his son. It was a beautiful situation because everyone benefited. The marriage stayed together and Jimmy healed. He went on to college, graduated, and became a CPA.

Some children aren't as lucky as Jimmy. They live in an abusive home where any feelings of anger can be met with rage or a hand across the mouth. Such children learn very early to keep all their feelings to themselves. This is the boiling caldron that can lead to addiction and abuse.

Counselors are also alert to the possibility of parer
ment in the child's problems. Counselors will ask if the
tinely compliment the child. We ask if the parents have ~p~... ...u~..
time with the child as he or she has been growing up. Other questions tend to zero in on possible parental problems. Do you feel you
could not please your parents? Do you feel your parents love you?
Is there any alcoholism in your family? Were you sexually abused as
a child? Do your parents do most things for you or try to spoil you?
Do you have feelings of shame for your mother and or your father
because of their alcoholic behavior?

Most addicts and substance abusers have a history of alcoholism
in their family and most adolescents are acutely aware of their parents' problems, even when parents do not perceive this. The dysfunction parents inflict on their children because of alcoholism is
even more devastating to those children who already feel insecure
about themselves. The shame experienced by an adolescent because
of parental alcoholism is greatly magnified during this crucial time
in their development when peer acceptance is so important. The
resulting feedback changes the behavior of the child to the point that
the child, too, may seek alcohol or drugs in an attempt to wash
away the pain by self-medicating. This exemplifies why some believe
that, while children of alcoholics have a tendency to become alcoholics themselves, it is not by genetics, but rather by the environment. In the question of nature vs. nurture, it is often the case that
a child of an alcoholic will learn from his or her parents what behavior to adopt in order to cope with the stress of life.

Many abusers and addicts also believe that money, success, and
power will help them to be liked or loved. Some of these adolescents
or adults did not have confidence in themselves when they were
younger. Their parents did everything for them as they were growing up; they stopped them from making their own decisions and did
not allow them to accomplish things on their own. These addicts felt
deprived. Other addicts felt that they were failures because they

could never please their parents. They were usually told so by their parents.

In short, addicts can become such out of their internal anger. While it is essential to recognize the root cause of the anger, and deal with it accordingly, keep in mind that ultimately we're simply talking common sense. What happens if, as an adult, you are unable to express your anger at work or at home? Divorce, violence, getting fired, "going postal" are results we're all aware of. There is a reason why we see it more and more. There is a reason why children have taken the lives of other children.

They are angry. Some are spoiled, and many are neglected. Some are spoiled with material riches, but have no adult to guide them. Some are spoiled and angry because their parents want to "be their friends." Some are angry over the size of their face, the size of a mole, or because they lost the part in the high school play or were snubbed in a lunch line. Some of the things that make children angry are silly and foolish and, when looked at logically, disappear like puffs of smoke.

But we cannot dam up the anger. Parents have to use common sense and spend time with their children. They need to discipline them, love them, and talk to them.

Over the years the greatest single source of anger among many of the children who became dangerous criminals is that their parents (specifically fathers, for most boys) were not around.

That should be easy enough to fix.

CHAPTER 4
Parental influences

*My child seems to be better off when I gave
him more space. I care, but I believe it is better
to let my child do his or her own thing.*

IN MOST HOME ENVIRONMENTS no one has more impact on a child
than the parent or guardian. All of us, in many ways we understand
and many we never understand, are products of our parentage. But
who are our parents and what decisions do they make that ultimately help us to become the people we are?

Certainly some parents teach tolerance, instill discipline, and give
love—some of the ideal traits we all hoped for from our parents, and
all hope to impart as parents ourselves. But the truth is that we're all
flawed individuals, far from perfect, who at times live out our ideals
and at other times fall short. Ultimately, our imperfections can affect
our children the same as our parents' imperfections have affected us.

When clinicians see parents it is usually not on the best of occasions,
and we try to take that into account when evaluating a family and how
its members interact. What we have seen leads us to believe that troubled children—and by this we mean children troubled enough to need
therapy—have parents who usually fall into three types: the *perfectionist parent*, the *enabling parent*, and the *apathetic parent*.

THE PERFECTIONIST PARENT. The perfectionist is usually the meticulous
parent, some would call the "anal retentive" parent, who usually
grew up in a household with a perfectionist as one of his or her parents. These parents are parents of extremes and are rarely satisfied.
Nothing their child does will ever be good enough. They prod, they
poke, and they generally push their children to try and be perfect. A

lot of parents who do this believe that by engaging in this behavior and setting extremely high and sometimes unrealistic goals, they are helping their child to succeed.

In some cases they are right. Setting high goals for some children and prodding them to great accomplishments can help children to succeed, and the attention that such a parent gives does make the children believe that their parents care for them. Logically, these parents believe that even if their children do not attain "perfection," whatever that is, they'll still be able to achieve great things in life. The child will do well and be that much more ahead of everyone else by having extremely high expectations.

But, of course, there is a downside to this. No one can attain perfection, and parents risk having their child constantly striving for the unattainable, and as a consequence, the child may never be happy. Ultimately the child may come to believe that he has a defect that keeps him from attaining perfection, thereby driving down his self-esteem, which leads to serious trouble. What the child doesn't understand is that the perfectionist parents are driven by an unfulfilled need themselves. Perhaps they are living vicariously through their children, hoping for them to fulfill the one dream the parents never fulfilled as children. Or perhaps the parent is suffering from his or her own parenting mistakes from childhood and passing on the parenting traits taught him.

The perfectionist as a parent usually starts off by setting up a situation where whatever the child does is not good enough. The message is always "you can do better." A project in school could have been better, if the child had put more effort into it. The child's performance in a school play could have been better. The hit that drove in a run could've been a home run only if the child had tried harder. For the perfectionist, nothing satisfies. A B+ is not as good as an A. An A isn't as good as an A+. The perfectionist isn't happy with a child's performance even if the child says he or she tried his best. The best, according to this type of parent, can always be better.

Some of this, as any parent can see, is necessary in trying to get a child to do his or her best. Every child "slacks off" on occasion and needs a parental reminder not to become lazy or indifferent. But the perfectionist goes too far, and soon the child comes to believe he can never satisfy nor please his parents. Some of these children struggle their entire lives trying to please their mother or father and feel like failures because they never can. In many cases, even when the child has reached adulthood, his parents have a hard time accepting him.

A quick example of this is the story of Fred and his mother, Mary. Mary and her husband were both attorneys. The husband became a successful judge while Mary went on to plead a case before the U.S. Supreme Court. Fred was their firstborn son, and while his two younger brothers eventually became lawyers like their parents, Fred did not fit in. He could never please his mother. His low self-esteem led him to bouts of anger and cigarette and alcohol addiction. He loved sports and wanted to be a coach, but sold cars and insurance to make a living, having never graduated from college.

He spent a lifetime trying to please his mother, sometimes bringing her newspaper clippings that praised his efforts as a coach and as a salesman. She wasn't impressed. She was the epitome of the perfectionist. To her, Fred was a failure because the firstborn son hadn't become an attorney like her two younger sons. The height of the snubbing came when Fred's father won reelection as a judge. At the celebration after the election, Mary stood up in front of a crowd and praised her two younger sons for helping out in their father's election campaign. She named both children—but completely ignored Fred. Although he had contributed as much as anyone to his father's election, he didn't exist to his mother.

Fred labored under the scrutiny and snubbing his entire life. He was twice divorced and while he had four children of his own and tried to take care of them, he was a "bad Catholic," according to his mother, and she even told anyone who would listen that he was destined for the nether regions filled with red-hot flames and the taunting of the devil's minions.

Fred eventually drank and smoked himself into an early grave. At his funeral his mother looked at her firstborn son and cried. "Maybe this will teach us all to accept one another," she said to her other children with all the pain and horror a mother feels at having to bury one of her own children.

Her realization came too late to make a difference to Fred, but perhaps it isn't too late for other parents.

Some children of a perfectionist simply give up trying, content to be failures because, after all, that's what mom and dad have called them for years. Others get so upset because they believe they have failed and start to feel hopeless and hurt themselves physically, or attempt suicide. These children have given in to the hopelessness their parents have mistakenly engineered into their lives.

The problem is that as children we tend to equate acceptance with love, which means from a very early age we will try to please our parents to get their acceptance and, ultimately, we believe, their love. If we can never please our parents, we are cast into a pit of emotional despair that is self-defeating and at the root of many dysfunctional families.

Many children who have the perfectionist as a parent get into abuse and addiction, like Fred did, as a way of taking a vacation from the pressure. The children have become so focused on trying to obtain the unattainable, or so emotionally distraught over the inability to be perfect, that sometimes abuse and addiction are the only options the child sees to escape the stress.

When we see perfectionists coming in with their children, we try to channel what at the root is a good, caring parent into a more positive role. It is best to get these parents to encourage their children without being judgmental. Perfectionists aren't usually neglectful parents, but hypervigilant one who usually learned their behavior from their own parents. If they can unlearn some of the bad habits of their own parents, such perfectionists usually react well to therapy, as do their children. With these parents and children we base most of the therapy on "progress" and not "perfection." The "Borg" in Star Trek are enamored with perfection to the point of sacrificing their humanity. We try to focus on getting better, or doing better, rather than perfection. This helps families out immensely. We can all get better and progress, and while we don't want failure as an option, nor do we want to stress families out trying to attain perfection.

Some perfectionists, however, believe they are pushing and prodding their children because the children are resisting any type of parenting. Their child is resistant, defiant, and doesn't want to put in any effort to progress or become better human beings. Some children, indeed, trigger the perfectionist by being recalcitrant or uncooperative; many often act out. The perfectionist, in this case, overplays the parental hand by substituting good boundaries with unrealistic and unattainable goals.

All children need boundaries. All children want them, and all children respect the efforts of a parent in supplying them, even if the child rebels against them. However, perfectionists need to understand that while they can ground the child, or give a small child a "timeout," or set other punishments for inappropriate behavior, setting those boundaries shouldn't be because the child has not attained some unattainable goal called "perfection."

Children can come to see a perfectionist as a cold, distant parent who is never nurturing and never loving. Strict disciplinarians are sometimes perfectionists.

THE ENABLING PARENT. The enabling parent is just the opposite. These parents believe the most important thing to do is to protect and nurture their child. It's normal and natural to want to nurture and protect a child, but again, like the perfectionist, the enabling parent is a parent of extremes. While the enabler believes he or she is providing a positive environment for the children, they are not. Instead they become doormats for their children, who end up ruling the household rather than the parent.

Many times these parents have very natural desires to supply their children with the best they can offer. Most parents want their children to do better than they did, and to have more than they had. But the enabler overindulges, thinking this makes them good parents—and, coincidentally, enablers believe they're taking care of and protecting their child with this overindulgence.

This overindulgence even extends to knowing their child is on drugs. In treating these parents and children we've seen the parents continue to give money to their child, even though the parent knows the child will probably use the money for drugs. The parent "cares so much" about his or her child that he does not want to see the child walking around without money.

Enablers, as we can see, are overprotective and unrealistic. They can almost always be seen rescuing their child from themselves. We've seen cases where the enabling parent will bail a child out of jail, pay the child's car payment even after the child has blown his money earmarked for the car payment on drugs. We've seen parents make excuses for their children's illegal and self-destructive behavior and we've seen parents add to the problems by doing so.

The enabler sets up a situation in which a child's negative behavior is rewarded, which is one thing a parent should never do. This helps the child continue in a spiral of self-destruction and makes it harder to reverse the process.

Take the example of Fred again. Fred, as we saw, had a perfectionist mother who demanded a certain behavior of her son. Her mantra was that her son could never "apply the seat of his pants to the seat of a chair for more than five minutes." If he brought home good grades, they were never good enough. If he achieved anything, it was never good enough. The things he treasured, his mother did not. On the other hand, his father was an enabler. Whenever Fred got in trouble with his mother, the father bailed him out. He loaned him money, he gave him support. The mother beat him down and the father propped him up. Fred never learned to stand on his own. He became an alcoholic and never achieved what he wanted in life.

Some enabling parents, because of the way they were raised, have a need to be needed. These are usually parents who have come from very dysfunctional families themselves and who get their own self-worth from how much their own children need them. For such parents there is joy and purpose in always rescuing their child and consequently never allowing the child to stand on his own. Unfortunately, some enablers also criticize their child for acting out in a negative or self-destructive fashion even though—and sometimes at the same time—they are bailing the child out. Yet because the parent is an enabler there are no consequences for self-destructive behavior, only criticism. This criticism is extremely unhealthy for the child because it usually isn't constructive in any manner. It is destructive and serves as a cancer on the soul, teaching children they are beyond redemption. A child learns very quickly to ignore the criticism and take the help.

Sometimes enablers come from a dysfunctional or alcoholic family. They reason that because they weren't given the proper attention, protection, and care they needed growing up, they will not repeat the syndrome when they themselves are parents. Again, this leads to overindulgence and a reinforcement of negative behavior in their own children. It is very difficult for enablers to break their habits, let alone understand that what they believe is good parenting is actually contributing to the problems their children are experiencing.

What we do is try to give the enabling parents a clear understanding of what unconditional love is and how it differs from their own behavior. Unconditional love includes what some have described as "tough love." The enabler has a hard time understanding that a child needs clear and definable boundaries. By setting those boundaries you tell the child you are not going to be a part of the child's destruction. We also try to teach the enabling parent that by constantly giving in when their child pushes, they are fueling their child's low self-esteem and not allowing the child to stand on his own two feet.

This is crucial for child development, but the enabler doesn't see it. Giving in continuously sets the child up as an adult who will constantly look for someone to bail him out of dire situations. At the same time, enablers who constantly criticize the child while refusing to set boundaries also set their child up for failure. Without the proper boundaries and with inadequate corrections the child can develop a guilt complex. If a parent always gives in to a child, and then criticizes the child's behavior, on a subconscious level the child believes he is a bad person and consequently needs to be punished, thus initiating the never-ending loop of destructive behavior. Healthy boundaries can help put an end to this problem.

To get an enabling parent to change his or her behavior it is good to treat both parents at the same time, if at all possible. If the parents come together and present a united front and learn from the education we've provided them, then they will be better equipped to stop their enabling behavior and set boundaries and consequences together. A united front, whenever possible, is essential because the child will invariably try to split the parents when dealing with them. This manipulative behavior can be quite successful, and an especially cunning child can be extremely difficult to handle. All parents know this much from having a child who will first ask one parent and then another in order to get his way.

However, it is sometimes difficult to get both parents together. One parent may be completely out of the picture because of death or divorce. A single mother or father will have an especially rough time if he or she is the only parent around and is an enabler. We try extremely hard to provide these parents with support through our therapy and services. In a one-parent situation, there is usually very little support for the single parent. We have sometimes seen other family members—grandparents, aunts, uncles, even new boyfriends and girlfriends of the single parent—step in and help. We encourage this type of participation whenever it is healthy for the child and the family. The essential goal in helping enabling parents is to get them to reclaim control of the family—control the child has wrested from them through manipulative and self-destructive behavior.

THE APATHETIC PARENT. Finally, another type of parenting that we often see is the apathetic parent. Today's fast-paced society, is, of course, a large contributor to this behavior. But it is only a symptom of a greater problem. Many times apathetic parents have forgotten the importance of a parent in a child's life. These parents can be found delegating authority whenever possible to soccer coaches, teachers, day-care centers, baby-sitters, and even neighbors. They simply avoid all confrontation with their children. Often this is because the parent has become so involved in a career that the parent cannot take the time to care for the child.

In these cases, it is not so much that the parents willfully turn their backs on their children. Rather, they believe they are doing the right thing by putting in the extra hours and guaranteeing an income and material advantages for the children. That is the seductive quality of a career and a job that eventually can get a parent to a point where the only support they provide their children is material in nature. This denies what can be most important to a child and most therapeutic: spiritual or psychological nurturing. Children want material possessions, but *need* to connect with other people and, specifically, with their own parents.

This need has been recognized in our fast-paced world, but has been deposited into our fast-food mentality. We often hear the term "quality time" to define the child's need in this regard, but such a description and attitude do not take into consideration that to a child the *quantity* of time put into the relationship can be more important in some cases than the quality of the time. When your son or daughter calls you on the phone or confronts you in the home and says, "I need to talk right now," it isn't healthy to put the child off with a comment like, "Well, I'm busy right now watching the game, but remember we have our talk time tonight before you go to bed."

Children pretty quickly come to understand where they fit on the priority list in their parents' life and it will appear not all that high, even if the parents believe otherwise. That isn't to say that a child should always dictate when and where interaction with their parents take place, it's just that they should not get the impression they are of less consequence than, say, the NBA semi-finals.

Sometimes apathetic parents also feel guilty and attempt to buy their way out with their children. Excessive gift-giving is an example of this. The upscale parent with cash to spare may not only give gifts often, but lavishly in the guise of credit cards, cars, cell phones, and so on.

Of course other apathetic parents just don't care about their children. They don't want the hassle for whatever reason. Some of these parents are extreme in their feelings, which appears as apathy, but can actually be jealousy. Some parents are jealous of the attention their children get from others. Some wish the children would go away. Some wish they had children at an older age. For whatever reason, they aren't involved and they can be among the most difficult type of parent to get into therapy. The mere thought of entering therapy to assist their children is too much energy for an apathetic parent to spend.

We have been able to defeat this attitude if we can get the parents to spend time in therapy where we reinforce the important role that parents play in their child's life. The apathetic parent comes to learn that getting involved with drugs is just a symptom of their child's deeper problem—the child needs parental nurturing and guidelines. This is especially evident in male children when the father is apathetic to his son. The boy needs male nurturing and, if he doesn't get it from his father, he will seek it out in others. In the drug culture boys will get that male nurturing from less than savory characters, i.e., their drug dealers and drug buddies, until abuse and addiction become the problem instead of the lack of male nurturing.

It all boils down to the fact that if your own parents don't want to spend any time with you, you're going to have some emotional distress, which can evoke a wide range of negative thoughts and feelings. Recent studies have shown that, on average, mothers spend about eleven minutes of that so-called "quality time" each day with their children whereas fathers spend only about eight minutes. It is easy to see how a child who gets such limited attention from his or her parents will opt for other stimuli, and the resulting stimuli may not be healthy for the child.

These are not hollow words. A recent study at New York's Columbia University showed that a father is indeed the key in keeping his children from abuse and addiction. Children who didn't get along with their fathers were 68 percent more likely to experiment with drugs than children in a supportive two-parent home. Remember those wonderful scenes of family life and a family sitting down to dinner in *Leave it to Beaver* or *Make Room for Daddy?* Well, it turns it out that a father sitting down for dinner with his children can help eliminate the desire to experiment with drugs.

Going a step further, the Associated Press reported in February 2001 that parents who impose strict rules on their teen-agers have a better chance of raising drug-free children. But guess what? Most parents set few or no guidelines at all. In today's politically correct world it is often said by parents that they want to be "friends" with their adolescents. The bottom line as far as kids go is that even if they say they want their parents as friends, they need to have parents who do the job of parenting even more than they need another pal.

It cannot be overstated:

> **IT IS IMPORTANT THAT PARENTS GET INVOLVED,**
> **AS PARENTS, WITH THEIR CHILDREN**

We have also found that specific-gender parenting is probably the most important parenting for children. That means that while it is important for a young boy to get attention from his mother, it is even more important that the father be present. Conversely, girls need attention from their fathers, but they must have more attention from their mother.

Boys need fathers. Girls need mothers. And both boys and girls need a father and a mother. Usually, especially in a young boy's case, if the specific-gender parent isn't available, the child may become what we call a self-saboteur. If a boy isn't getting the nurturing he needs and feels his father doesn't care for him, he will go through life sabotaging his own chances at success. He will set up situations that look like he's successful or going to be extremely successful, and all of a sudden he will act out in some way to sabotage the success. We've seen boys go all the way through school with National Honor Society status and suddenly act out at the very end of high school, sabotaging their career in some cases so thoroughly they aren't able to graduate. The journey from the National Honor Society to a high school drop-out seems extreme, but we've also seen children blow college scholarships and travel farther down the road of despair, not only dropping out of high school, but becoming substance abusers and addicts.

For some parents it may be hard to understand how they are involved in their child's problem—especially if the cause of the child's problem is so far removed and seemingly unrelated to the parent's activity. So, a parent, specifically a same-gender parent, who criticizes or ignores a child will be hard pressed to understand why the child always self-destructs the closer that child gets to success. When a parent of the opposite gender is the criticizer you will not often see a fear of success in a child nor self-sabotaging behavior, but you will see a fear of failure that can lead to an unhealthy obsession with perfectionism. These children are extremely stressed and often pathologically fearful of failure.

Whatever baggage the child brings to the table, the antidote is to listen to the child and make sure the child feels comfortable talking to the parent. Don't act out. Don't get angry. Speak quietly and be inquisitive. Take, as an example, this conversation, which actually occurred between a father and a son about the son's homework in school. The son approached the father about leaving home when he knew he was supposed to be doing his homework:

FATHER: Do you have homework?
SON: I have to go up with Mom to get something at Office Depot.
FATHER (QUIETLY): So, do you have any homework left to do?
SON: No, uh, I have to go up with Mom to get a binder at Office Depot. Mine's broken. (The "uh" in the conversation is always critical. A parent must explore that.)
FATHER: Why do you have to go with your mother to Office Depot?
SON: I want a new binder.
FATHER: So, that's not homework. Other than that, do you have any homework left? (pause) Okay, this is what I mean when I talk about communication, son. I have now asked you three times a simple yes or no question and I still haven't gotten a yes or no. Do you have any homework left to do?
SON: (pause) Well, yes.

The parent has spent a little bit of time exploring the inner workings of the pubescent mind, yet maintained control of the situation. The pubescent wants to control everything. It's best at an early age to discourage irrational attempts at control. This is best done directly and without anger. Calm logic can make its point even to the pubescent.

Meanwhile, a perfectionist child driven by a either father or mother is usually stressed out and becomes so overwhelmed with the stress he may not try to succeed at all. The fear of failure becomes so great he simply gives up before trying. This reinforces their already low self-esteem and they drift into drugs to literally "feel no pain."

They self-medicate.

Years ago we had a client who was a beautiful woman and an editor of a newspaper in a major metropolitan area. She had very little contact with her father, and when she spoke with him he was always critical of her. Although a very successful journalist, she was an even more successful drug abuser. She felt ultimately she was never good enough, everything she ever did wasn't good enough for her father. This, of course, caused a lot of emotional distress, so much so that the same woman who was interviewing major local political players by day, was in questionable areas of town scoring and shooting heroin by night.

She struggled for years with this pain and was never successful in overcoming her desire to please her father. To this day she is in a long-term rehabilitation program.

Finally, it should be noted that all of the types of parents we've discussed so far are not necessarily the worst for children. The worst-case scenario parent can be any of the types we've discussed already, but also something much more horrific. The worst parent is physically, emotionally, or sexually abusive. Unfortunately, by the time we see a lot of children, some type of abuse or neglect is already going on in the family. We have seen the self-worth or the self-esteem literally beaten out of kids by parents who do not know how to parent correctly. These parents usually carry a lot of anger around with them and many times are children of abusers themselves. The physically abusive parent sets into motion a whole string of potential outcomes, none of which are favorable, and which are often extremely destructive. Some serial killers, for example, have been found to have had neurological damage inflicted on them by abusive parents.

The most insidious part of abusive parents is that they play to a child's need to trust an adult and, specifically, a parent. When we are small we rely on our mother and father to keep us safe and secure. We know not to stick our fingers in a light socket, or play in traffic and other essential safety rules because of our parents. Naturally, we learn to trust their decisions, so that when a parent becomes physically abusive in the name of punishment, children get the wrong idea. They begin to think they are "bad" people. They will actually act out and seek punishment to verify these feelings that they are "bad," which only fuels the cycle of abuse.

Also, as people grow up and believe they're somehow defective or "bad," they will suffer extremely low self-esteem and act out in ways to get attention and punishment. We have seen kids who were severely physically abused at a young age continuously break the law and use drugs to escape and soothe the trauma of their abuse. This escapism becomes full-blown addiction.

We cannot stress enough how devastating physical abuse can be. We had one fellow in our clinic who remembered his childhood as a series of beatings administered by his father. The father made the son kneel naked in the yard. Beatings would follow. As the boy grew up he moved into the drug culture, self-medicating to get some kind of relief, and hanging out with drug dealers to get the male nurturing he didn't get from his father. He used cocaine and heroin intravenously. At one point, high on drugs, he ran down his neighborhood street naked and then into a church, begging God to forgive him for being such a bad person. Eventually this client developed AIDS and died tragically young. At the root of his despair and short life were the beatings and humiliation he suffered from his own father.

Sexual abuse is another terrible extreme of bad parenting. Children suffering from sexual abuse have the hardest roads to travel. They feel a great deal of guilt and shame, which erode all feelings of self-esteem. Prisons are filled with people who have been abused physically, mentally, and sexually. The common thread running through all of those who have been abused is the guilt and the shame. Many who have been abused feel they are defective. Many blame themselves for being abused and feel responsible for having initiated the harm that befell them. Many adolescents who have been abused act out in a variety of ways. Men may become abusers themselves, whereas women tend to become promiscuous. But some women who have been sexually abused learn to use sex to control men and others in their life. It becomes the one thing they feel they can control. Most of the prostitutes I've interviewed had been sexually abused as children.

We've also found that many borderline personality disorders are the result of sexual abuse. Again, these people carry around a lot of guilt and shame. They feel guilty and believe they've done something wrong, and so deserved to be punished. This sets up a situation in which the person continues to act out in a negative way. He then feels guilty, seeks punishment, and the cycle continues. This insidious condition, if left unchecked, can lead to death. The abused feel they are bad. They feel guilty. They must have done something bad. Bad people deserve to be punished. "I was doing drugs and that makes me a bad person. I feel guilty. I took drugs." On and on it goes.

People who have been sexually, emotionally, or physically abused also have a hard time developing lasting relationships. Those take a certain amount of trust and the victim of abuse finds it hard to trust anyone. Sexual abuse can also lead to sexual identity crises, especially if the abuser is of the same gender as the child victim.

Some boys who have been sexually abused by an older male start to question their sexuality. This causes unbelievable stress and a lack of confidence. Some men who have been traumatized by older women in early life will have a hard time having a meaningful relationship with a woman when they get older. Because of their trauma they cannot trust a woman and are unable to be intimate with anyone in any type of relationship.

On the other hand, some women who were sexually abused by their father or other older males became lesbians because they feel they cannot trust men. They never really develop a close relationship with another woman, however, because they feel they cannot trust anyone. The statistics back this up. According to the research findings of the National Lesbian Health Care Survey, more than 21 percent of all lesbians said they had been abused as children and 15 percent said they had been abused as adults. Other findings showed that lesbians reported higher rates of alcohol problems than heterosexual women and that the heavy drinking didn't decline with age, as compared with heterosexual women.

The stress on these children is almost unbelievable, and the results are clear enough for anyone to see. When it comes to children, as we said at the beginning of this chapter, no one has more influence on their life than the parent.

The sobering reality is that many parents today don't know or don't care. The results are warning signs for the rest of us. Parents have to be more involved in good activities with their children if we are to have any hope of curing some of the societal ills we watch in mute fascination on our television sets every night.

CHAPTER 5
Egomania

My child seems horribly self-obsessed.
The only thing he ever talks about is himself.

IN WHAT AMOUNTS TO A BIZARRE CONTRADICTION, those with the lowest self-esteem often become ego addicts and appear to the rest of us as overblown, superconfident extroverts who relish the spotlight. They boost their intensely negative self-image by controlling others, often through fear and drugs. The "cool" and grandiose street dealer is but one example of an ego addict. A child who brags to others about violence could be another example. The drug dealer gets his high by making his customers cower and grovel for the drugs he sells. The violence addict gains his high by making his peers cower and grovel in fear.

The ego addict, in short, uses power over others to reinforce his fragile ego and compensate for his inferiority complex. By involving himself in risky behavior associated with criminals and dangerous felons, he proves to himself that he is in control.

Joining a street gang, with its image of power, is yet another way the ego addict can achieve this end. Joining a gang will also give the child with low self-esteem a feeling of belonging and love. We are dealing here with mostly young men who believe that no one could like or accept them just for themselves. They are very sensitive to perceived insults. "Don't dis' me, man," may be the last verbal warning before a fight or gunplay takes place in the world of gangs, and there's a reason for it. The members of most youth gangs have egos that are so fragile that the least little bit of criticism or lack of cooperation can lead to violence. It's a very unhealthy and volatile environment for a child.

Children who belong to street gangs are wearing a big sign on their brows screaming for love, parental involvement, discipline, and true friendship. Their egos are so shattered and the need for ego sustenance so severe that joining a gang for many is a last chance at some kind of human contact, nurturing, and ego nourishment.

Ask most street gang members why they joined a gang and they will tell you it was for survival. The big question is why packs of undisciplined youths must band together to survive. How does it help them survive, and how can we stop it?

The problem extends to young women as well. An ego-addicted male can be used by those in power, or may utilize power himself to achieve some ego nourishment. A special problem, though, can arise when an ego-addicted young male comes across a young woman with low-self-esteem who isn't necessarily an ego addict but is male-dependent.

This type of young woman tends to be dominated through fear and abuse by the ego addict. The young male ego addict often accumulates such young women as trophies. Thus you see numbers of young women who seem to be attracted to the ego-addicted gang member or drug dealer. Young women in such predicaments feel they cannot be loved or respected as individuals. Suffering the effects of low self-esteem, they rarely seem to be able to separate themselves from their abuser.

How low self-esteem works on an ego is extremely complicated. A person of low self-esteem who is addicted to the rush of ego may come to see the dealer on the street corner as a man of wealth and discriminating taste—certainly independent. The young ego addicts may also witness their father abusing their mother, or other stimuli that makes them believe that power over others is a way to defeat the bad feelings they have about themselves.

It is very dangerous when adolescents dream of power and obsess about having power over others in order to defeat low self-esteem. The drug culture is filled with these ego addicts. Plenty of dealers are in the drug trade strictly for the money, but others constantly feed their ego by feeding others drugs. These are usually the lower level dealers, who themselves are being used by larger dealers, but the low-level street dealer obsessed with power doesn't see that. What the dealer sees is steady customers depending upon him for drugs. The ego-addicted drug dealer derives from them a sense of accomplishment. The dealer sees people coming to him as beseechers and begins to believe he's "cool." He hears people call him "The Man." He's the man with the plan, and when his customers have the need, he's got the speed. All the hubris and macho posturing, even the seemingly necessary and totally superfluous violence, cannot hide what is, at the core, a very wounded and troubled individual who doesn't think much of himself.

Be on the lookout as a parent for a child who suddenly has a roll of cash on him for no apparent reason, or is suddenly buying nice jewelry, nice clothes, or even a car while working the grill at the local fast-food restaurant. Something is definitely wrong with that picture. The child may be belligerent and evade questions should they turn to money or spare time. These too should be tip-offs for a parent.

By the time a parent becomes aware of this problem, other ancillary ones may be cropping up as well. A child who knows he is doing wrong by dealing drugs, but has gained some measure of self-esteem from it, may develop an attitude that it is "better to reign in hell than to serve in heaven." These children can become increasingly dangerous to themselves and others. They will take great pride and pleasure in embellishing their status through power and control. These are the repeat offenders who are constantly in trouble with the law for drug dealing and eventually other crimes, which may or may not be violent.

Again, the root cause of their criminal behavior is their low self-esteem, but it is unrecognizable in a child who is dealing drugs, doing drugs, robbing, and thieving. They see their customers as the real lowlifes, groveling for drugs and doing anything to supply their habit, and while the dealer may be engaged in the very same behavior as his customers, he will invariably distinguish between himself and his customers by virtue of the power he has over them.

We have treated a lot of young men in this position. They are highly egotistical and need to fuel and feed that ego by abusing and manipulating other people. We've seen these young men use and abuse young women in every way imaginable and we've seen these young women accept the abuse as long as the drugs flow. The young women get a rush from the drugs and the young male dealers get more of a rush from watching the women grovel for the drugs.

The combination of a low self-esteem drug-dealing male and a low self-esteem drug-using female is perhaps one of the saddest things to see. Many of these people grew up with low self-esteem. They come from a variety of environments: rich and poor, well educated and poorly educated. The only constant in their lives is the low self-esteem. Ego addicts without the fix of power and control will soon fall back in on themselves. Depression and suicide are possible, as is violence.

What the parent must realize is that the ego addict, while appearing arrogant and aggressive, is really hollow and shallow. They cannot help themselves or don't want to help themselves. Many times, even if they do want to help themselves, they can see no way out of the box in which they've placed themselves. Most of the families and adolescents we've treated for this behavior come from physically, sexually, or emotionally abusive environments.

This brings us to a girl named Frannie. She was absolutely beautiful. She was also kind and sweet—a very good person. But Frannie had a severe addiction to cocaine and was also male dependent because she had a physically abusive father who rarely spent time with her unless he was harming her.

She also had one dealer she visited consistently. He was constantly degrading Frannie and was a big ego addict. Frannie, who had just turned eighteen, was being horribly manipulated by the drug dealer. He had videotaped her in lurid sexual poses and sexual acts that he forced Frannie to perform. Aside from the sexual gratification he got from the pictures, he kept these videotapes as a reminder of how cool he was and how much power and control he had over Frannie.

This went on for about a year until Frannie ran out of money and her dealer became bored with her. The only way Frannie could score drugs now was by selling off her possessions. The first thing her dealer wanted was her prized possession, a new sports car. She gave it up by reporting it as stolen. Her drug dealer took it and sold it to a chop shop.

Soon Frannie found that even giving up her prized possession couldn't secure the drugs she wanted, so she decided she would steal an eight-ball of cocaine from her dealer—three and a half grams. Her attempt was unsuccessful and the resulting beating and rape by her drug dealer finally convinced her to get serious about therapy. The downside was that she determined she never again could trust a man, nor sustain a relationship with one. Although she eventually was able to separate herself from the ego addict, she retained wounds she could never heal.

Thus it is with ego addiction.

Michael was also an example of the problem. He sold drugs for years in New Jersey and after being arrested three times it was mandated that he get into treatment, and he came to us.

He seemed to be successful at treatment, going onto recover and becoming a counselor for other addicts. The problem was that Michael, while seeking treatment for his alcohol and drug problems, never sought nor knew enough to seek treatment for his ego addiction. It was still out of control. Michael kept it in check as long as he was able to nourish his ego by counseling other addicts, but he never addressed the emptiness he felt inside.

This finally caught up with him when he decided to go into business for himself. Recognizing a need, he became a bounty hunter for different rehab facilities. If an addict was looking for a facility, Michael would hook him or her up to the rehab center for a fee—paid for by the rehab center.

At first Michael was successful and his business grew steadily. In seven years he had amassed a fortune and even opened up his own rehab facility, all of which was feeding his ego addiction. But nothing was enough. He had to be bigger. He had to have the biggest rehab facility, the most patients, and the greatest service.

While on the outside it looked like a good thing, inside it was taking its toll on Michael. He still didn't feel good about himself. Finally, Michael got into trouble because he was brokering human beings like cattle and sending addicts all over the country to different rehabs just so he could pocket the money. He ended up sending patients to rehabs that would pay him the most. Eventually, of course, he was arrested.

In the end Michael couldn't face the stress. As his court date got closer he began using drugs again and descended into a heroin haze from which he never recovered. He overdosed and died weeks before the trial.

Michael and I met two years out of recovery, and while Michael was an extremely nice guy, it was obvious he had troubles. He had a low self-esteem level and he found he couldn't literally buy good self-esteem. He tried.

Of course ego addiction isn't limited to the drug and violence trade. Corporate executives, politicians, actors, and anyone in the public spotlight has to have a bit of an ego. But the unhealthy ego is the one who can *only* feel important as long as the audience is clapping and sending praise and kudos—sometimes even boos. Still, as long as the ego addict is getting *something* from the outside, he believes, inside, he is all right.

Without the outside stimulation the ego addict can become depressed and descend into narcissism and rage. To catch these ego addicts early on, before they become adults with larger problems, is hard for a parent. After all, a healthy ego is a good thing, and parents strive to encourage their children to excel and succeed. *But parents need to be on the lookout for the warning signs to see if their child is trying to be a people-pleaser or using money or status to have power and control over others. Also be on the lookout for children who use mental or physical intimidation as a means to an end.*

Ego addiction can take many forms. Some may be as socially acceptable as the president of the United States, others can be as dark as serial killers. Environment and upbringing can shape the form of the addiction, but, remember, the ego addict is always under stress. They constantly need to feed their ego.

Many men who abuse their spouses may be ego addicts. They are severely narcissistic and usually use drugs and drink. They want total dominance, power, and control over their wives. They need to feed their ego continually with their dominance. They've been known to kill their spouse before they'll let them leave them.

Tom Capano, the social scion of Delaware who was tried and convicted of killing one of his nineteen mistresses, Anne Marie Fahey, was like this. He had money, power, and attention, but needed more. Nothing was ever enough for him, and he was empowered by his mother, who told him he was the "pearl" of the family.

When Anne Marie told him "no," he snapped and killed her rather than allow her to go on with her life.

Remember, ego addicts are fed early in life. They are extremely fragile. Many male ego addicts, although they appear macho, are fragile and, like a glass case, if you jostle them just a little bit, they'll shatter and you'll see the egotistical rage rush out.

Frequently we've dealt with the ego addict in counseling. They all share a few things in common—their ego addiction fuels their self-esteem only for the length of the stimulus. In other words, ego addicts only feel a rush, like the rush of a drug, when they are engaging in activity that heightens their self-esteem.

Ego addicts mistakenly believe that self-esteem comes from without and all of their activities are geared toward stimulating their fragile egos. Violence, overachieving, drug addiction, power over women—these are activities directly linked to the ego addict with low self-esteem.

David Koresh, the leader of the Branch Davidians who engineered a standoff with the FBI that led to his death and that of dozens of others—including women and children—in Waco, Texas, is but one famous and extreme example of an ego addict gone horribly awry. He had a healthy messiah complex and indeed said he was the "dirty Messiah" who had come back to earth to have sex and use his power as he saw fit. Men and women became enamored of his power and flocked to him, only to face their doom at his hands.

Take a good look at the next person you suspect may be an ego addict. Is he or she so obsessed with power that it is causing other aspects of his life to be unmanageable? In children, look for the need always to be the center of attention, to the point that rooms aren't clean, homework isn't done, and grades falter. When you try to communicate with the child face to face, is it as if he or she is ignoring you, as if you weren't there? Does the child lack empathy with others? Ego addicts often cannot see others as people who can suffer pain, but like chessmen to be moved about for their own ends. Look out for the child who believes he is entitled to everything. A child who believes the world owes him a living is a good tip-off that something is amiss in that child's psyche.

Finally, women are as susceptible to ego addiction as men, but the way our society has been geared until recently in our history, it has been extremely difficult for the female ego addict to manipulate the levers of society to her own end. Today, ego addicts can be found in all walks of life, from the board room to the back alleys. They are drug dealers, bookmakers, gang members and leaders, pimps, and womanizers but can also be found lurking in more upstanding careers from cops to lawyers to doctors to politicians.

The ego addict is a fluid individual, chameleon-like (or strives to be), who can operate anywhere. Because ego addiction isn't illegal, like drug addiction, and is in some ways much more socially acceptable, it can be very hard to identify and treat.

After all, who wants to raise a child who doesn't have a healthy ego? The problem is that parents have to provide adequate safeguards, discipline, and love to make sure a child with a healthy ego doesn't turn into an ego addict.

CHAPTER 6
Genetic aspects

My husband says he got into a lot of trouble when he was younger and dismisses my son's behavior to genetics. Is there any truth that genetics plays a role in low self-esteem or addiction?

CERTAINLY MANY SCIENTISTS AND DOCTORS believe there is some sort of genetic predisposition to drinking. Some at this very moment are looking for the elusive "alcoholic gene" in the human genome. And on the face of it, there seems to be sound reasoning for such a search. It is well documented that close to 50 percent of all alcoholics have alcoholism in their family. Of even more interest is the fact that 96 percent of all cocaine addicts have alcoholism in their family, according to a Rutgers University study.

Researchers have spent millions, if not billions of dollars of taxpayers' money on research to find the gene that causes alcoholism in support of the theory that it is a disease. But I personally don't think they'll ever find such a gene, because I'm not sure such a gene exists. To begin with, alcohol is a very toxic substance in the body and the body goes to great lengths to try to expel alcohol quickly and efficiently. To find a gene that causes a craving for alcohol is tantamount to looking for a gene that causes a craving for arsenic or some other toxic chemical.

There is also the dynamic of cocaine and alcohol. Alcohol is a strong central nervous system depressant, whereas cocaine is a central nervous system stimulant. Yet an overwhelming majority of cocaine addicts had alcoholic parents. It seems inconsistent for a gene that could cause a person to be predisposed to craving alcohol to also make a person crave cocaine. However, the research is sure to go on and money will continue to be spent.

In the meantime, there are other ways to treat dependence and they are not based on genetic models. Low self-esteem is prevalent in drug and alcohol abusers years before drugs are used. A person walking around feeling he is somehow not as good as others does not need a defective gene on which to blame his pain. There are plenty of factors in the world outside of the person to influence someone's self-worth. The reason why children of alcoholics become alcoholics or cocaine addicts is often because alcoholic parents do not provide the nurturing, care, and responsible discipline that a child needs. The child of an alcoholic may therefore become an alcoholic not because of genetic disposition, but rather because of a lack of parenting inherent in the alcoholic mind-set.

Certainly, as we've discussed, a vigilant parent—one who is there mentally, physically, and emotionally for his or her child—is less likely to raise a child who will be given over to some form of abuse or addiction. Drunk parents find, if they care, that they are in an uphill battle, unable to support a child's needs. It just can't be done. With the alcoholic comes angst and often physical, verbal, and mental abuse. The trauma that a child undergoes in this type of household may be all that is needed to turn a child into an adolescent or adult with low self-esteem and the predisposition to abuse drugs as well.

There are plenty of tales of children "pulling themselves up by their bootstraps" who overcome such an upbringing, and perhaps that, in itself, is testimony against any genetic predisposition to abuse and addiction. But the numbers also indicate that *something* is going on in an alcoholic household.

The key to treating these problems is not to take a "cookie-cutter" approach to them. It is extremely popular in therapy today to generalize and treat each alcoholic or drug abuser as if he or she is part of a fast-food franchise. This is not only lazy therapy, it can lead to more harm than good. The therapist must strive to get inside the minds of those being treated and inside the family dynamics.

What appears to be a genetic problem may in fact be one of the many behavioral problems we've already outlined. There may also be other problems. Many are looking at genetic triggers for neurotransmitters that have a known effect on the brain. These neurotransmitters help pass information through the brain and all psychoactive drugs interfere with the normal delivery of information by the neurotransmitters.

For example, acetylcholine is a well-known neurotransmitter that affects memory. Synthesized by Baeyer in 1867, it was first noticed as a compound that lowers blood pressure, increases peristalsis, and was identified as early as the 1950s as the substance released from nerves to activate the muscles. It's also involved in focus, attention span, and learning ability. If children have a depletion of acetylcholine they're going to have a hard time paying attention and remembering things. They'll have trouble with both long-term and short-term memory and they'll also have problems with concentration and attention span. When children are not doing well in school because of a depletion in their acetylcholine levels, they can end up in special classes or even special schools.

Riding the "retard bus" to the "weird school," as some of our clients have labeled the experience, is something no child willfully wishes to experience, yet they not only must take part in such activities, they are chided by their peers for doing so. Alcohol depletes the acetylcholine levels, as does cocaine.

Another neurotransmitter in the brain is dopamine. Some scientists believe dopamine may hold the key to some types of alcoholism. Dopamine appears to play a very dramatic role in an individual's mood and, without an adequate amount, depression follows. Chronic dopamine shortages can be the cause of serious depression.

Some with depleted dopamine levels can suffer Parkinson-like effects. The term "punchdrunk" used for boxers refers to the Parkinson syndrome displayed by Muhammad Ali. Hard-using drug and alcohol addicts will display symptoms remarkably similar to this; in fact, it has been shown that alcohol and drugs deplete the body of dopamine. At the end of an addictive cocaine cycle the addict faces depression. The same thing holds at the end of an alcoholic's destructive run: depression. And, inevitably, low dopamine levels.

Norepinephrine is another neurotransmitter that can cause problems. It enhances motivation, learning ability, and assertiveness, and assertiveness problems can lead to low self-esteem or depression. Remember, low self-esteem is a precursor to depression.

Drugs available on the market now address some of these shortages.

With all of this said, it is still a far cry from saying there is an "alcoholic" gene that directly causes alcoholism. *It perhaps could be a defect in a gene,* but consider that alcoholism is responsible for a wide variety of toxic ailments—kidney disease and heart disease, for example—and it is hard to believe that the human organism would evolve a gene that destroys the organism.

We've seen people come into our clinic with high blood pressure, or pancreatitis, or heart problems, and always, after the medical history is taken, we find alcoholism or drug abuse involved. Again, what organism would create a gene that would cause a craving for a substance that would destroy it?

Isn't it more rational to try to find out more about the individual involved in the therapeutic process and tailor treatment to that individual's need(s)? At our clinic we do not believe in a fast-food approach to treatment. Handing out a pill doesn't cure all emotional ills, nor does putting a person into a group setting—which may be the most profitable for the clinic but may not be so therapeutic for the person. These ideas have ruffled some feathers, but we've come to believe that, as doctors individualize physical treatment, so must the therapist individualize treatment. Talking, searching, and finding what is at the core of a person's distress has had much better success, we've found, than the fast-food approach.

With that said, serotonin, another neurotransmitter, can be involved in alcohol and drug addiction. The lack of serotonin causes insomnia or fitful sleeping episodes, and alcohol and drugs deplete serotonin levels.

So, again, although genetic triggers may be involved in alcohol or drug addiction, it does not mean a gene will cause addiction. There are stories of addicts who can stop using on a dime; we've seen this happen. We've seen hard-core alcoholics completely stop ingesting their drug of choice simply because they chose to do so.

President George W. Bush told a national audience that he decided to quit his excessive drinking because his wife gave him a choice of Jim Beam or her, and he wisely chose his wife. He didn't drink again.

This all lends credibility to the idea that those with alcoholism in the family will tend to be alcoholics. But they probably do not have a gene that predestines them to be such. People can and do change their behavior when they are aware the behavior is self-destructive and if they have enough self-esteem to want to do things that will benefit them and not destroy them.

But children who have grown up in the home of a drug addict or alcoholic will invariably carry with them scars of those times that were brought on by the dilatory effects of the drug their loved ones were ingesting. These may be emotional as well as physical scars. Interestingly, children whose step-parents were abusive have shown as much predisposition to becoming alcoholic or addictive as the biological children of alcoholics and addicts.

In fact, merely growing up in a home where an alcoholic lives, whether related or not, can be cause for concern. Again, this would tend to call into question the notion of a direct genetic link to alcoholism and instead point to the behavioral influences of those nearby as having an effect on the individual.

In other words, you know what you experience and see. You learn from it and act or react to it. As a child, if you grow up in a home where there is an alcoholic, you will probably suffer emotional if not physical abuse. You will be yelled at, you will be demeaned, and your self-esteem will be called into question every day. But that does not mean you are necessarily going to end up doing the same thing to your children or others. You can decide not to. It's that simple, but people sometimes have problems committing to that notion.

There are those who believe that direct physical trauma induces anxiety and depression, and may deplete neurotransmitters. Part of our treatment lies in trying to determine if there is trauma underlying the low self-esteem we see exhibited by addicts and abusers. Because if there is, then chances are self-respect and confidence have been compromised. It's hard to feel good about yourself or have any confidence in yourself if you are constantly being belittled, berated, or beaten.

Physical trauma also compromises intimacy and intimate relations. Trust is violated and abused, and it therefore becomes hard for the victim to regain trust for anyone. Sometimes merely surviving as a child in an alcoholic family is a miracle in itself. A child will manage to survive an alcoholic family, but by the time the child gets to us, he or she has such a shattered psyche that surviving and existing are about all the child can do. Thriving and growing, trusting and loving are concepts wholly alien to many of these children.

It is important, therefore, to get to the parents as quickly as possible. It is also important for parents who come from alcoholic families and have a predisposition to addiction to know that they do not have to raise their children the way they were raised. Many times parents know nothing more than what they were taught by their own parents, and even if they are loving and giving parents and aren't addicts themselves, they can still repeat the bad behavior of their parents. In this way they can continue to pass the stress and strain from addiction on to their children, causing problems in breaking the cycle of addiction.

Therefore, the bottom line in all of this talk about genetics is that the best way to treat the problems of addiction and abuse is still through better parenting. *Vigilant parents are kind and loving and listen to their children, but are still solid disciplinarians who are more concerned about being parents than being their child's friend.* Vigilant parents may be friends with their children, but are more concerned about being good parents.

We also know what our parents did that was right. We need to select the best and toss away the rest. But to do so means that, as parents, we not only have to be involved with our children, but think before we act. In the heat of the moment when a child does something incredibly stupid, or incredibly horrible, a parent may act before thinking. In doing so, chances are the parent is going to act out the way he or she was taught by his own parents. If an alcoholic parent was involved, chances are the action may not benefit either the parent or the child.

As the parent goes, so goes the child. But we are more than just the sum total of experiences given to us by our parents. We are more than the sum total of our genetic makeup. We have the ability to think and change our behavior. It is extremely important as parents that we instill self-confidence, self-respect, and a high self-esteem in our children.

That is ultimately the argument against the "drinking gene," for it does what we've endeavored to do as a culture for many years—take responsibility out of our hands. In the case of behavior, it is always up to the individual, the whole organism, to make changes. A gene cannot dictate how a parent will react. It cannot make you drink. It cannot make you treat your children badly. It cannot compel you to do that which you know is detrimental to yourself.

Looking for the magic bullet or "drinking gene," therefore, can be a crutch for those who do not wish to take responsibility for their own actions. "It's not my fault, it's all in the genes," goes this argument. In the end it is another excuse, another denial, and taking that path is not salvation but slavery to addiction and abuse.

Parents must think. Parents must act upon the knowledge they have. Parents must be involved in their children's lives. Genetic predisposition be damned.

You are the parent. You can make the difference. If you want to.

PART II
TYPES OF TROUBLE

CHAPTER 7
One addiction, many forms

It all seems so confusing. Are there common threads involved in addiction? What should I be looking for in my child's behavior?

THERE ARE A VARIETY OF ADDICTIONS, but really only one source, and to find it we must take a look at what all addictions have in common. It is correct that many of the addiction problems we've discussed have similar symptoms. They are all part of the same disease: low self-esteem.

We've outlined the causes of low self-esteem and talked about some of the problems that can stem from them. Now, let's take a closer look at the specific addiction problems. Addiction, whether chemical (e.g., drugs, alcohol) or behavioral (e.g., gambling, co-dependence, violence), is a self-destructive illness. No matter what form it takes, the addiction controls behavior and overrides normal social instincts. Addicts will cheat, lie, steal, or manipulate others in any way necessary to feed their habit. Addiction robs the addict of free will.

Most addicts have a difficult time identifying and expressing their feelings. Their feelings can be submerged under too much alcohol or too many drugs, or avoided by being directed toward someone or something other than self—a loved one, or gambling, for example. The result is that addicts often lose their sense of self, of identity.

All addictions are obsessive-compulsive disorders. The addiction, whether chemical or behavioral, is a way of substituting an obsessive fantasy or good feeling for painful, real-life issues and a sense of inadequacy. The substitution can take many forms: alcohol, drugs, gambling, obsession with a loved one—anything that negates the underlying stressful emotions associated with low self-esteem and whatever helps the addict to feel more alive.

Most addicts eventually get to the point where their lives have become unmanageable. Perhaps an obsessive-compulsive person becomes so focused on cleaning that she does nothing but clean, or is convinced that nothing can be clean. Another victim of low self-esteem may become a heroin addict who never bothers to bathe. So, while perhaps a Manhattan Upper East Side clean freak who spends all day vacuuming and worrying about pleats in the draperies may seem to have nothing in common with a homeless heroin addict begging for enough money for a daily fix, both have much more in common than they realize. They are victims of low self-esteem. One may be more functional than the other, but both have had their lives taken over by their addiction.

Most addicts progress from an experimental phase to an abuse and dependence phase before progressing to outright addiction. The trip may be a short one, or it may be long. We could be talking about the gambling addict who might begin as a weekend poker player, or a visitor to Atlantic City who gets his or her first thrill with four aces or hitting a jackpot. We might also be talking about the future heroin addict who got a heavy rush from injecting heroin for the first time. But it was that initial rush that lured them outside of themselves and gave them a giddy feeling of euphoria that they will chase thereafter. Think of the obsessive shopper who gets off by finding a pair of shoes on sale, or the aforementioned clean freak who felt "just for a moment" that everything was "great" when she got the apartment clean. It is the same feeling of escape and release that the gambler or the drug addict chases after.

Eventually the experimenter becomes the abuser and soon they will feel their lives are unmanageable. Many kids with low self-esteem who come in for treatment who've gotten involved in abuse start to feel some of the negative ramifications: school failure, arrests for possession, sometimes distribution and dealing, DWI's or DUI's.

Sometimes they get into trouble by stealing or shoplifting. Robberies can occur—whatever it takes to get the money to obtain the substance they are abusing. Sometimes they'll steal from themselves, selling off a cherished possession that will purchase the illegal drugs or sponsor the gambling that will help ease the pain of their low self-worth or depression. Perhaps they will take that prized possession and give it to someone else, someone the child is obsessed with, in order to ease the same feelings. It can take many different forms.

Low self-esteem is a wicked beast and feeding it can lead down a deeper and deeper hole and feed back on itself. When the addict begins to lie, cheat, steal, and manipulate to ease his or her pain, that is when the feedback begins.

ACTING OUT to feed the low self-esteem is when the low self-esteem becomes noticeable. Teens become guilty about their actions, and acting out only reinforces their lack of self-respect. A teen may not even notice that he or she is doing it. This is the critical time when low self-esteem can spiral into depression and begin feeding on itself.

In the beginning of the process, an occasional dalliance into drugs or gambling isn't as dangerous to the child, but it is seductive. Heroin addicts often say they never recapture the feeling they got on their first "high." Forever after they are chasing that initial rush, and can never get it. This is often the case of addicts who've spiraled into depression from low self-esteem, no matter what the substance they are abusing. Gamblers report similar feelings, as do those who are co-dependent. They don't recognize that the initial high, the first rush that makes them feel so good, is transitory. They do not understand that it's a false sense of hope and that they've just taken the first step down a slippery albeit rocky slope.

As their grades fall and they have more problems with their parents, police, and friends, the young addicts get more and more down on themselves and never realize that the cure they sought through drugs or gambling or something else has become the greatest cause of their spiraling depression. By the time they do, if they ever do, it may be too late. They've become self-criticizing and negative about themselves, and therefore need the substance to quell their painful and stressful feelings.

Keep in mind that, as this circle continues, the need for money increases and there's no way an addict can be totally honest. They will lie, cheat, steal, or manipulate in some way in order to feed the addiction.

One example is a young boy by the name of Joey D. When he came to us he was using heroin, but was only sniffing it. When we got to the bottom of Joey's low self-esteem, we found that he thought himself inadequate and inferior. He grew up with an alcoholic father who was hypercritical of Joey from a very early age. Joey was always told he was bad and would never amount to anything. So Joey walked around with tremendous feelings of guilt because he was such a bad person.

Joey eventually got into heroin and received immediate relief. When he sniffed heroin he didn't feel the pangs of guilt. But he grew tolerant to the heroin and he moved on from one to two to three bags and eventually up to ten bags of heroin a day. In order to get the money to feed his habit, Joey began shoplifting.

Of course, Joey then felt guilty about his shoplifting and heroin abuse, which just reinforced the feelings of guilt from early childhood. He was feeling guilty about stealing, about everything—that he was an addict at such a young age, that the effects of the drug were keeping him from doing even the simplest things in life. While other kids were socializing, playing football or soccer, going to the mall, studying, having fun, and doing the million other things kids his age are usually doing, Joey was anaesthetized from heroin—literally, in some instances, unable to move.

Joey's ritual went something like this—all addicts have rituals and they may differ from one another, but they should be recognized as ritualistic behavior:

Joey would go out and steal. He would score his heroin and feel no pain. Then when he came down from the high he would have intense feelings of guilt, which caused him emotional anguish. He also felt physically ill because of his tolerance to the drug, and thus the ritual would start all over again. This continued until Joey got caught shoplifting at the ripe old age of seventeen and was brought to us for treatment.

"The more I use the guiltier I feel and the more I use," he told us. We explored that with Joey and eventually he came to recognize the feedback loop in which he was caught. After our evaluation, we sent Joey to rehab for forty days. Then he came back to us and we began therapy. At this point Joey was motivated to clean up and he gained insight into the root cause of the guilt feelings that had led him into the drug culture.

He came to realize that the guilt had been put on him by a drunk, angry father. He broke the cycle of drug abuse when he gained a higher self-esteem. He woke up. He went back to school and graduated and moved on to college.

Joey certainly is a good example of the "one addiction, many forms" concept. He could have been addicted to anything. He chose heroin. Only when he became aware of the root cause of his addiction was he able to change the patterns of behavior that led him into the cycle of depression and addiction.

When Joey came to us and said, "I refuse to be my father's whipping post. He has his own problems," we knew that Joey had begun to see the light and realized that he had allowed his father to destroy his self-esteem over many years.

No addict becomes an addict from the heights of high self-esteem. No self-obsessed stalker, no gambling addict, and no child addicted to violence ever became dangerous because he thought well of himself. Who in their right mind becomes dangerous or engages in self-destructive behavior out of a sense of well-being? Obviously no one. Even a child who claims to love violence for the sake of violence becomes violent out of a sense of despair. You can even look at the Oklahoma City bombing in such a way. Until his very death, Timothy McVeigh tried to play the role of martyr for the cause. But what cause was it he was preaching? You must get past what is on the surface and what is being sold in the media to truly understand how and why we are losing our children to drug abuse, violence, gambling, and other addictions.

McVeigh is the worst-case scenario. His story is supposedly well known, but little is made of his deficiencies because we concentrated only on the horror of his actions. This is not to make excuses for him, but rather an attempt to understand why someone would act in such a way and correct someone's future behavior before it manifests itself in something as tragic as the Oklahoma City bombing. We cannot accept at face value the reasons McVeigh gave for his destruction because they fly in the face of what we know caring human beings do to one another. We cannot accept that he was healthy, any more than we can accept that a heroin addict is healthy. So how do we embrace those who seem to be evil and seemingly do not care about their fellow human beings? It seems at times to be a task beyond most of us; indeed, by the time a child has chosen and fallen into his self-destructive addiction, it can be too late.

A vigilant parent is an involved parent and must come to realize not only the root causes of addiction, but also that addiction comes in many forms. Parents often become so upset about the symptom—i.e., drug addiction—that they become too overwhelmed to deal with the root cause. But there is another insidious possibility that families must also confront. Parents may want to deal only with the symptom because they do not want to confront the harsher reality. The reality is that often there is something amiss inside the family dynamic. We see this many times in a clinical setting. Children traumatized by physical, emotional, or sexual abuse are brought in by their parents because of a drug problem. The parents want the drug problem cured, but don't want to deal with the fact that they are part of the problem.

Parents want to keep the focus on the child because they don't want to deal with their larger problem. Sometimes children also want to keep the focus on themselves because they're afraid that if the larger family problem is dealt with it could disintegrate the family.

This is when the therapist must be very careful. We have to focus on the child's problem and stabilize the abuse or addiction. Then we must identify the root cause of the child's low self-esteem and, after scrutiny of the family dynamic, encourage the parents to try to deal with the larger problems. If you include the parents who spoil their children, in almost every case when we see and treat a child we find that a larger and deeper family problem is behind the child's problem.

The vigilant parent will want to be a part of the cure, but often we see parents who do not. This problem inside the family dynamic is the single largest problem we face in trying to treat younger children in our clinic. Sometimes we actually see children act out in order to get their entire family into a setting where the family can get help. In these cases the children's low self-esteem, fueled by their parents arguing, or emotional abuse of each other or the children, has forced them to act out to the point that the children need therapy. But children aren't stupid, and they'll use the clinical setting to try to get their parents, who also suffer from low self-esteem, into our clinic for help. Their lives and the lives of the members of their family have become unmanageable. It is amazing, sometimes, to see how a child will reach out to try to bring some measure of manageability back to the family by intervening in such a manner.

Others whom we see in our clinic also come in once they've reached a point in their life when they cannot manage their day-to-day needs. Compulsive gamblers are but another example of this. They start out with recreational gambling just as the substance abuser starts off with recreational drug use. As their lives become unmanageable and their low self-esteem fuels and reinforces their negative behavior, they will began the feedback loop that compels them to continue gambling. When we get the compulsive gambler in our clinic, even teen-agers, it is only after the addiction has brought about some dire consequence—arrest, incarceration, a visit from the not-so-friendly shylock, and so on.

Gambling and co-dependence are seemingly different, but dependent upon the same things to make them happen. Usually in co-dependence a loved one chases them into our agency. Usually that person has a low self-esteem problem himself and needs to be needed.

The reason for some of the programs like Al-Anon is because of the enabling that takes place with loved ones of alcoholics. Many times the person closest to the alcoholic has, in ways they may not be aware of, helped their loved one become an alcoholic or maintain his or her alcoholism. The co-dependent person is as addicted to people as much as other people are addicted to substances. These twelve-step groups help the co-dependents find independence.

It's easy to see how low self-esteem plays out in the life of co-dependents. Their focus is totally on others and usually only a bit on themselves. We've seen co-dependents being so dependent on their loved one that they've ended up going through the same physical and emotional stressors that the addict does. They'll develop heart problems, high blood pressure, anxiety, stomach problems, and they'll become very depressed. It's very interesting to see a co-dependent family member. They'll begin to spiral downward into despair or depression, even though they're not involved in drugs themselves. They'll lose their self-respect the same as does the addict. They feel guilty because their loved one is going down the tubes into drugs.

Most of these co-dependents never recognize they're undergoing the same problem. Abandonment issues arise and they cannot see they're addicted to another person; they're too focused on pleasing, because as long as they're pleasing someone else they're not going to be criticized. Their egos are so fragile because of their low self-esteem that they become the people-pleasers who never recognize they're part of the problem and not the solution.

And it's all being fueled by low self-esteem.

The point is, as long as they concentrate on someone else, they don't have to focus on themselves. They are distracted from reality. They are addicted to people. Their drug is people. And they mainline it as surely as a heroin user does.

Marge threw Tommy's father out of the house. He was a verbally abusive father, a physically abusive husband, and a violent alcoholic. Marge always felt guilty about this and so became overprotective of Tommy, struggling to be a father and a mother to him.

She started early on to indulge Tommy and give him whatever tangible things he wanted. Yet she also felt the need to criticize him when he did things that were wrong. She became a constant criticizer while at the same time spoiling the boy with material goods. And all the while she carried around the guilt of putting Tommy's father out. She focused completely on Tommy. She became co-dependent. She spoiled him. She criticized him.

Tommy, thus, was never allowed to accomplish anything on his on. He never gained confidence by learning through experience how to accomplish anything. He never had any confidence. He moved into substance abuse, got caught on a urine test in high school, and came to us for counseling.

We assigned a male therapist to assist him and he seemed to be responding to the nurturing and therapy. Marge then said her son was fine and pulled him out of treatment But she continued her old patterns and Tommy fell again into his self-destructive habits. Her reasoning was that as long as Tommy needed her, she had a job. She didn't want Tommy to become independent because then Tommy would leave her and she'd end up alone.

Thus, she always sabotaged Tommy's counseling and any attempt at independence. This was all on a subconscious level. She was not vindictive. She honestly cared for her son, but she had her own low self-esteem problem.

She began to see she was doing her son a disservice, but couldn't break her bad behavior. Finally Tommy got arrested with seven marijuana joints in his car and was forced back into treatment. We told the court that the treatment would be fruitless unless the mother underwent counseling. We got them both into counseling and Marge realized her addiction to her son and began to change her behavior.

At the bottom of all of this is the abuser's need to ease low self-esteem through addiction. It takes people away from themselves so it eases the stress; it medicates the person who cannot deal with low self-esteem and depression.

It's a comfort zone that addicts believe will help them deal with everyday life. The only way to work through this is to talk about it and get people in touch with the real motives for their actions. Feelings are often hard to understand and harder still to overcome.

What it all breaks down to is that self-criticism leaves people feeling bad about themselves. And thus they must have medication. It can be obsessive-compulsive behavior or dependence. We can call it habitual, like habitual gambling. They all turn around and reflect the same situation: Addiction.

Addiction is co-dependence, obsessive-compulsive behavior, habitual gambling, and drug addiction with low self-esteem at the root of it.

We have taken a look at the signs of trouble and the foundations of addiction and abuse. Now we need to take a look, more closely, at the types of trouble that a child can get into because of low self-esteem and how those problems play themselves out.

Remember, as we look at these problems, the root cause is the low self-esteem that led to the depression, that led to the addiction—no matter what form of addiction it takes in the individual child.

A parent will have little success until he or she realizes that even the most flagrant and mean-spirited or self-destructive behavior has at its base the need to be loved and the fear that no one actually cares about the addict. This fear, this need, and the outside stimuli of abuse or neglect are what produce the low self-esteem and addiction we see in such high numbers today.

CHAPTER 8
School violence

I'm scared my son is going to do something drastic.
I don't think he'll kill anyone, but he has talked about it.

OF ALL THE THINGS A CHILD CAN DO that is harmful or dangerous, today the drunken teen, or the drug-addicted teen is not what we adults and parents fear. Today, alongside our fears of terrorism, we fear the child addicted to violence, the child who fantasizes and eventually acts out in a manner that may end in a public display of death and suicide for the disturbed child.

As we noted in Chapter 3, internalized anger can be a very dangerous thing. But what we would like to look at here is a specific type of anger that seems to be more apparent now than in the past: mass violence in public areas.

For children, the venue is most likely to be the school they attend, and thus we see scenes like those outside of Denver and San Diego. School shootings are, as previously stated, the worst-case scenarios of internalized anger, and it is worth looking at the specific warning signs for this problem.

To put it bluntly, many times the signs were there to be seen, but apathetic parents allowed the signs to go unnoticed. Perhaps the parents were ignorant of what the signs meant, or even in denial.

Clearly, any time a child is speaking about bodily harm or violence a parent should stand up and take notice. Let's take a closer look.

When we look at these kids, we see children who have been abused many times in one way or another, which sets them up for low self-esteem and the frightening aspects of teen-age depression.

Whether the abuse has occurred through family, friends, neighbors, boyfriends or girlfriends of single spouses, or perhaps at school through excessive teasing, the obvious observation is that many children involved in school violence have been victims of abuse and many suffer from extremely low self-esteem.

They feel rejected by peers or family members or friends. This is at the core of the anger and the rage we spoke of previously. Anger has been dammed up and unable to flow.

The central thing to remember about a child who is so involved in anger that he actively plans to carry out the act of mass murder is that the situation didn't just pop up overnight. It wasn't because the child didn't get a ride to school, or wasn't treated nicely at a school dance. The child who commits such an act has been ignored, neglected, and abused for years. The act of violence, much like the hoary cliché says, is a desperate and last cry for help—usually before the child kills others and ends his or her own life. A child with this mind-set is a child wrapped up in a cocoon of pain who can find no way out.

That many of these children are from the middle or even upper-middle class is not inconsistent with this theme. Many of these children are latch-key kids in some fashion, and neglect and abuse cut across socioeconomic lines. From all of our research, kids who abuse other kids or who become violent with other kids have been abused themselves. It is not unlike the behavior we see in adult serial killers.

That is not to say that some children in these situations do not find ways to cope. Some children find healthy ways to divert their anger despite a lack of parental care. Some find sports, others religion, and still others become socially active in many different ways. These children have found, either through their own initiative or by observation or advice from outside, a way out of the cocoon.

Unfortunately, some children cannot find their way out. The children who cannot cope are those who eventually fall into a core of despair. They are lost, disconnected, and neglected, and seek any kind of human connection, meaningful and loving if possible, but murderous and hateful if that's all that's available to the child.

These children may eventually become completely disconnected from reality. Nothing seems real, because they feel they have nothing anyway. A child manufacturing pipe bombs in the family garage shouldn't be discovered only after a murderous rampage. That type of child may feel everything is so unreal that even manufacturing bombs is unreal. If it were real, the child may reason, someone would stop him. Surely his parents would notice. That no one does notice or stop him only fuels his addiction and depression.

Obviously these children in some cases have a real reason for feeling disconnected from the rest of the world: they are. Their parents ignore them. People may pick on them. They feel unwanted, neglected, and unloved.

I once heard an educator say, "Parenting is the lost profession of our generation," and perhaps for the aging baby-boomers that is true. Perhaps we were so good at rebelling against our parents we forgot the best things our parents taught us. Certainly there has been great cause for consternation because of the violence in our schools and the alcoholism and drug addiction of our children. A vigilant parent will want to reevaluate his own behavior as his children grow and their needs change.

But whatever the cause, there seems to be a complete disconnection between parent and child in today's world. Finding volunteer adult staff for youth activities has become increasingly difficult over the years. Youth organizations across the country are constantly looking for parents to become involved in football, soccer, basketball, and other youth sports programs.

Teachers, educators, and coaches all have horror stories of parents who merely drop off their children. Entire cottage industries have been built around the need for after-school care for children, not to mention preschool, nursery school, day care, and extended care. Parents from the earliest age are subsidized for bad parental behavior. Can't get home? Don't worry, you can rent a parent for mere dollars.

Many school systems make decisions about the children in their care with the assumption that the parents won't be involved in the process. In an earlier chapter we discussed a fight that broke out between two young boys in Maryland. In that specific case the school system had in place a mechanism for counseling both boys that did not include the parents. When both sets of parents asked to be involved in the process, the school counselor was taken aback. She informed the parents that "parents were never involved" in the counseling.

A child who has no outlet for his or her rage is going to act out on that rage somewhere. Those parents who care sufficiently to look at warning signs for impending violence should look for physical bruises on their child. Is the child being bullied or abused? Is the child in a lot of fights? Look for radical changes in a child's behavior, or the unwillingness of the child to talk. A sudden change in friendships and manner of dress should also be revealing.

A vigilant parent needs to know that if a child who has always been neat and clean suddenly comes home dressed as a member of the "Trench Coat Mafia" there might be something wrong. Look closely at all aspects of your child's behavior.

Scrutinize the drawings of your child and the books that he or she reads. Limit and monitor the time your child spends on the Internet. Boys have a tendency to doodle at an early age. Drawing a tank battle or a fighter plane engaged in combat may not be anything to be worried about, but, again, take the time to ask the child why. Why did the child do that? What is going on? Encourage the child to keep the river of emotion flowing.

If the child withdraws from his parents, or if the child is less responsive to parental stimuli, find out what is behind this behavior. Kids who may move into violence not only suffer from low self-esteem and depression but are feeling despair and a sense of hope-lessness brought about by their disconnection from the rest of the world. That child will withdraw and may eventually seem like a complete stranger to his parents and everyone around him.

Defiance can also be a warning sign. Not doing the assignments from parents and teachers or fighting for no reason can be internalized anger trying to find a release.

Drugs and alcohol, as always, should be investigated, but the potentially violent child will also seem to be obsessively interested in weapons or cults. The family who has guns in the household would be well advised to lock up all weapons when they are not in use and make sure that the child cannot get access to them for any reason. The National Rifle Association's recommendations for safety should be followed, but better yet, don't give the child the temptation.

Cult interest can bring about feelings of gloom and doom and pump the young adolescent mind full of thoughts about violence. Dismemberment, impalings and graphic scenes of death are all standard attractions in most cults and yet another way internalized anger can be released.

This item appeared in "Shoptalk," the online magazine for journalists on March 15, 2001:

> In the wake of the Santana school shootings, nearly two-thirds of Americans believe that the best solution to stopping violent crime among youth in schools is for parents to become more involved in their children's lives. [emphasis added] And, an overwhelming 77 percent feel that media coverage of school shootings has increased violence, possibly motivating kids to "copycat" crimes to achieve notoriety. This according to a national survey conducted by E-Poll (www.epoll.com)—the website where Americans go to express their opinions on today's issues and trends. The survey, conducted March 10-12, 2001, offers an up-to-date,

statistically significant snapshot of Americans' views on the topic of school safety. More than 1,600 people participated in the survey. Other key findings of the national school safety poll include: In your backyard? 85 percent of those surveyed believe that an incident like Columbine or the recent Santana shootings could happen in their community schools. Thirty-seven percent are taking precautions to protect themselves or their family from random violence at work or at school. Crime and punishment: The majority of respondents (57 percent) say that parents should be held legally responsible for the actions of their child if he/she commits a school shooting with a weapon taken from the parent. And 73 percent feel that children under 18 who commit violent/deadly crimes at school should be tried as adults. How could this happen? According to the survey, Americans believe the top three factors that drive a child to commit a violent/deadly crime at school are:

#1 - Lack of involvement/communication with parents

#2 - Being bullied/intimidated at school

#3 - Access to guns/weapons.

Unfortunately media coverage and all popular culture seem to have desensitized children to violence. But again, at the root, we are staring at inadequate parental involvement, or, at the very least, inappropriate parental involvement.

In retrospect, with most of the high school violence being committed by young men, it becomes incredibly easy to wonder where the fathers are. Well, look around and usually you will see that someone involved in this type of violence has a very poor relationship with the same-gender parent—the father.

Apathetic parenting is at the bottom of most of it. What we know for sure based on the information from the FBI and others is that intense planning is involved in these events. If parents are not neglecting their children, are not apathetic, and are keeping a vigilant eye on their child, this planning will not go unnoticed.

When we're dealing with adolescence, we are also dealing with a lot of hormonal factors. It is well documented that adolescents do not think the way adults do. Sometimes they even believe they are immortal, and it's obvious from the criminal and risk-taking behavior of some children that they may only become aware of the consequences of their actions after they go over the rage threshold and kill or hurt other people.

Adolescents may understand that what they are doing—violence or drug addiction, for example—is wrong, but they are so enraged and so hell-bent on revenge that it clutters their thinking process. This is another risk factor and warning sign: watch for frustration, anxiety, and hatred in your child. "I hate you, Mom (or Dad). You're always interfering in my life," is not nearly so hard to take and understand as the child who screams in rage, "I hate you, Mom (or Dad). You're never around."

Finally, there will come a time when the enraged child can no longer turn back. He has organized and bragged about committing a violent event and, if for no other reason than to maintain his already strained credibility among his peers, unleashes his rage.

A child who brags he's going to shoot up the school, and doesn't, may find himself at a greater risk for teasing and put-downs. Fear of being called a punk, a sissy, a bullshit artist, may be more real and painful to an adolescent than the reprisal of killing a bunch of his peers.

Thus, the critical phase of a child's descent into violence is when he begins to talk about committing such an act. As it turns out, speaking thoughts of violence seems to help prepare the child for committing horrible acts of violence. So remember the cliché that "many a truth is said in jest," and even if a child seems to be joking about violence, a parent must be vigilant enough to ascertain if it truly is a joke or if the child has a darker desire. Childhood peers and acquaintances also must be tuned in to the child who promises violence, and educators need to encourage children to speak up. No child wants to stand up in the middle of class and be labeled a "snitch" for telling a teacher his or her classmate is talking about "pulling a Columbine," but the child needs to be encouraged to do so in a discreet manner.

Once the enraged child starts to talk about committing an act that might boost his ego or self-esteem you must act to intervene.

How that intervention takes place will be discussed later. Suffice it to say here that this could be the only chance to make a difference. The window of opportunity may be very small, but it will probably exist.

As males we are sculpted by our environment to be Gary Cooper in *High Noon*. We take care of business and we show no tears. Nice work if you can get it, but in reality men, and especially adolescent boys, have as many emotional problems as anyone else. Unfortunately for the way some young men are raised, there may be no release available for those emotions.

From the very beginning of life, the macho swaggering that has come to be a cliché has also been taught as a reality. "Big boys don't cry" and "tough it out" are told their sons by many parents. A child who has been taught to dam up his emotions and at the same time is dealing with an apathetic, neglectful, or abusive parent has a tremendous handicap to overcome. The risk of an emotional implosion or explosion is very great in these cases.

But remember that, ultimately, the child addicted to violence is a child acting out of depression and low self-esteem. These children may or may not be doing drugs. They may or may not be alcoholics or co-dependents or gamblers or excessive shoppers. But their anger river has been dammed, and having no way to vent, they blow.

These children prone to violence feel cornered, with no place to turn. What is left for the child to do in order to divert his or her feelings? It is obvious in retrospect that many children prone to violence got there because they felt horribly alone, and not just the normal anxiety that we've all felt. These children are so isolated by multiple problems—such as feeling physically unattractive, not being athletic, being a below-average student, having nonattentive parents, or having no friends, poor clothes, poor hygiene—that they feel trapped.

Sometimes these children will try a variety of other methods to soothe their feelings and escape their reality. We'll touch on the other problems of addiction in the next few chapters, but what we must learn here about the violence addict is that he or she feels cornered. We all know what happens when you corner a frightened animal, and it is the same with many of these children. They have reached a new level of rage that is the product of parenting and society. It is a challenge we must meet in this new millennium; otherwise, we face horrible consequences.

CHAPTER 9
Chemical addictions: drugs and alcohol

*My son says the only time he ever feels good is
when he's drunk or high. What can I do about that?*

WHEN WE SPEAK OF CHEMICAL ADDICTION, or chemical abuse, in a lot
of ways we are looking at a situation where the abuser-addict is
using a psychoactive drug such as alcohol to soothe the feelings of
inadequacy, inferiority, or insecurity that set the child up for low
self-esteem or depression. From this we get the term "self-medicating." The child is hoping to dull the senses, flatten out her emotional
lows, and bring stability to her life. "Better living through chem-
istry" is her fundamental goal.

As we pointed out earlier we can easily get to the core of the problem when we begin questioning the child who is abusing chemicals.
Once we find she is using chemicals to "feel good" we chase that
statement to its logical conclusion. The child doesn't feel good without chemicals and will explain why she doesn't feel good *if given a
chance*. This is key and where many parents fail their children. If the
children have been given a chance to explain why they don't feel
good about themselves and are encouraged to speak at will and at
length about it, chances are they wouldn't need therapy.

We often find that even the most distant children are actually
craving an outlet for their feelings. It may be tough to find a trigger,
but once found, the children will come forward. This is essential in
treating them and preventing them from spiraling down in their
depression to a lethal end.

Usually we find that the chemical being used or abused breaks down
inhibitions. This can lead to all sorts of edgy behavior, but the vigilant

parent must understand why the child wants to lose her inhibitions. Almost always, what the child is trying to do is to take away her inhibition. In other words, these children are doing their level best to take themselves out of reality—more importantly, the reality that is fueling the low self-esteem and depression.

When we find that a child is abusing or addicted to chemicals, we focus on three categories of chemical addicts or abusers. They are *depressant addicts, stimulant addicts,* and *fantasy addicts.*

DEPRESSANT ADDICTS. These children are usually trying to numb themselves. Their self-medication route takes them from low self-esteem and depression straight through to denial. In order to maintain this denial they want to numb themselves, usually with alcohol or perhaps other more powerful central nervous system (CNS) depressants. This can ultimately end in death if not treated.

Bill King, a stand-up comedian in the Washington, D.C., area, jokes about how alcohol advertisers should be required to tell the truth about alcohol. Essentially, his truth is that alcohol impairs women's judgment. He says it with a smile and he gets a laugh, but he is in many ways correct. Alcohol is a powerful CNS depressant that can act as a general anesthetic. It can also remove inhibitions and relieve emotional pain—especially low self-esteem. At least in the short run. But those who abuse alcohol, as we all know, get into a vicious cycle of depression, which leads to more drinking, which causes more depression, which eventually becomes an addiction.

But, in the short run, it can help your socialization, so if you're on the hunt for a girl, need to bolster your courage, eliminate stress, and induce a false sense of power, liquor may be your drug of preference. Other CNS depressants are also warning signs of low self-esteem. (Symptoms of the abuse of CNS depressants are covered in Chapter 1.) But should a parent find that a child is abusing opiates like heroin, codeine, or morphine, the parent should understand that the depth of depression can worsen and the problems with low self-esteem can be exacerbated by the use of illicit drugs.

It is quite easy to procure alcohol. It is somewhat more difficult to find heroin. Therefore children who are addicted or abusing heroin or other harder-to-find CNS depressants are probably not only deeply into depression and low self-esteem, but also may be harder to reach. Their denial may be monumental, their self-esteem nonexistent, and their potential for harm to themselves and others immeasurable.

The social acceptance of alcohol makes children who abuse it harder to get into therapy because adults and children look at alcohol as partying, socializing, having fun together. Parents may have a glass of wine with dinner. Adults go to sporting events and order a beer or two. Alcohol is pervasive, and very little stigma goes along with excessive drinking. In fact, in our movies, our commercials, and elsewhere in popular culture, beer and alcohol are dramatized as making you "cool" or "macho." Drink beer. Have fun. Get chicks, become popular and cool is the overwhelming message in commercials. A child can look upon a beer as his ticket to fun, frivolity, and even dignity. The reality, of course, is drink too much and you end up in a most undignified position, or getting in an automobile accident or assaulting others. Still, in print and in film, the casual drunk is not derided nor belittled but celebrated.

In short, having a family member who is an alcoholic may be stressful, but having a relative addicted to smack is quite another story. If your parents have a syringe-full of heroin with their evening meal instead of a beer or a martini or two, you have more than addiction and abuse to deal with. Usually, when CNS depressants other than alcohol are involved, there is more of a pathology at work. A stronger CNS depressent is not socially accepted. Picture having a drink, then picture tying your arm off and using a syringe. This indicates a stronger emotional need to become numb in an extremely dangerous way. There are more overdose deaths from heroin than from alcohol.

Again, however, the bottom line on all of these CNS depressants is the numbing and inhibiting effect that takes all angst and fear out of a person's life. Much has been said and written about the "rush" from taking these drugs for the first time, and indeed some addicts have said they continued to take heroin and other dangerous CNS depressants to try and recapture this "rush." But what caused them to take the drug in the first place, and what was their behavior while on the drug? The "rush" effect, as it turns out, may be a very shallow explanation for doing CNS depressants or any other drug. There may be a glimmer of truth in it, but it's far more likely that it is the numbing effects of the drugs they're after.

After shooting up, a heroin addict is nothing if not a living study of numbness. They just sit there, sometimes barely moving, sometimes nodding, or passing out. These people are anesthetized to the point of total numbness.

Ask the serious drunk, or ask the heroin addict what they feel and chances are they will tell you, "I feel nothing," they say. Some are quick to follow up with "And that feels good!" It is exactly where they want to be. All of their fears, problems, and the rest are gone, and "nothing" suddenly looks pretty good. "Sometimes nothing is a pretty cool hand," said Paul Newman in *Cool Hand Luke*. When you have nothing you have no anxiety, no depression, and nothing to worry about. The problem with that, of course, is that if you take it to its logical conclusion, feeling nothing can lead to suicide or accidental death.

STIMULANT ADDICTS. Just as dangerous as the CNS depressant abuser is the chemical CNS stimulant abuser. These people want to deal with their self-esteem problems in the opposite manner from the depressant addict. People addicted to stimulants want to be up, up, up, and up. They have a lot of energy and they want to feel stimulated so as to find their escape. They prefer not to have a down, numbing affect. To them that is the same as low self-esteem and depression. They want to be the life of the party. Some of them want to be the party all by themselves. Only in that way can they avoid their feelings of insecurity, inadequacy, or inferiority.

The stimulant addict is edgy and evasive, and others may see him or her as funny and outgoing. But it is all a mask to hide the pain. The mask is made of drugs and the pain is depression and low self-esteem. Stimulant addicts are not just addicted to chemical stimulants, but many times to anything that will stimulate their senses. Sky-diving, kayaking, mountain-climbing and rock-climbing are all sports that can attract a stimulant addict. Then, of course, there is sex.

Hypersexuality and constant arousal are high on the stimulant addict's list of participatory sporting events. Ironically, however, because of all the drugs they've ingested, stimulant addicts may not be able to perform sexually because they will not be able to get ample blood flow to consummate the act, if they are male. The first clue girlfriends and wives may have about their husband or lover's addiction could be summed up by a statement many of them have told us in therapy. "He wants sex and he can't do anything about it."

Children who have become stimulant addicts may not yet have that particular problem to deal with if they've not yet become sexually active. But the young stimulant addict may also be a young adrenaline freak attracted to extreme sports and peripheral activities that seem to make no sense. I once knew of such a child; his chief method of having fun was to run across a crowded secondary street filled with onrushing traffic. The closer he came to getting hit by a car, the better he liked it. He was also addicted to speed and had several altercations with his mother, since his father had died at an early age, leaving him and his mother alone.

This and other problems can cause the stimulant addict also to ingest CNS depressants. "Taking the edge off" is what the stimulant addict or abuser labels such activities. A cocaine abuser will therefore engage in "speedballing," cutting the cocaine with heroin. It is that ugly drug combination that killed the talented comic actor John Belushi. Sometimes the stimulant abusers take the edge off so they can perform sexually, and other times because they are trying to find a happy medium.

Stimulants take these people too high. Their heart pounds, their blood pressure rises. They're flushed and can begin to feel horribly uncomfortable. Then they'll drink or perhaps smoke pot or take something else to mellow themselves out a bit. They'll also do this so they don't "crash" from using the stimulants. Stimulant addicts who are suddenly coming down from cocaine or amphetamines find themselves in a pit of despair. They feel horrible and dirty, and they often look pasty and feel clammy. That is why they will often stay high for an incredible amount of time, or until their money runs out—they don't want to "crash." Alcohol can take the edge off that horrible experience, too. Yet when the alcohol kicks in, the desire for the stimulation remains, and so the abuser or addict will hit himself with another round of CNS stimulants.

It is an unhealthy and ugly roller coaster ride to the highest highs and the lowest lows. Those who get caught on this ride can be particularly dangerous as they search for the happy medium they will never find abusing chemicals.

FANTASY ADDICTS. The third kind of chemical addict is the fantasy addict. This type of addict can set up his or her own fantasy world via hallucinogenics like LSD, PCP, psilocybin (magic mushrooms), mescaline, Ecstasy, or even marijuana, hash, and hash oil. They want to escape reality but, unlike the stimulant addict who wants the rush of adrenaline, or the depressant addict who wants to be numbed into slumber, the fantasy addict wants to take a "magic carpet ride" to a world of his or her own creation.

They may mix and match chemicals, sometimes adding CNS depressants or stimulants to their psychotropic soup, but what they really like is to lead the Timothy Leary lifestyle cliché and "turn on, tune in, and drop out." They also favor acid rock and acid fashions and believe they've found deep inner meaning in the lyrics of Iron Butterfly and Pink Floyd.

Fantasy addicts may seem anachronistic, but they may also be easier to treat in some cases than other addicts, for there is little or no physical detox involved in helping them move on to recovery. The problem, though, is that these drugs may cause some brain damage, and a lot of psychological withdrawal can take place, such as paranoia, depression, and psychosis, for example

Michael is an example of this type of addict. A smart child, Michael got great marks in school and had even been called a genius by some. He excelled in math and got a scholarship to a prestigious university. But Michael had a secret and a problem. His problem was that he had been sexually abused at an early age by friends of his family, and Michael's parents weren't aware of it. That was part of Michael's secret, as was the fact that he was dealing with his problem by taking hallucinogens.

When Michael came to see us it was because of a problem with smoking marijuana. We got it under control for a while and Michael joined Narcotics Anonymous and stayed clean until he went into college. At that point Michael gave up going to therapy and quit going to NA meetings. He never did deal with the problems that came up because of the sexual abuse, or at least in no cogent fashion. Instead, once in college and away from home he began to get deeper and deeper into hallucinogens. LSD was his drug of choice and he was found one night leaving his home naked, and at another time crawling around on the floor naked.

Michael eventually lost his scholarship because he couldn't keep up with his school work. His condition continued to deteriorate, despite many attempts to reach out to him, and eventually he ended up in a state psychiatric hospital for long-term care. We never heard from him or his family again.

The sexual abuse that led to Michael's low self-esteem and

depression ended up destroying him via the fantasy world Michael sought through the use of LSD.

But again, much more familiar to many of us is the alcoholic who self-destructs in a similar manner. We have treated hundreds, if not thousands of those sad cases. Usually it takes about fifteen years for an alcoholic to finally wake to the problems of alcoholism. But, undoubtedly, the problems begin in childhood. We've seen men and women come into our clinic drinking anywhere from a quart to two or three quarts of liquor a day. And they always tell us they began drinking in childhood.

How the alcoholism can destroy the family, and the tension and potential danger of the affliction is shown poignantly in this poem one of our children in therapy wrote:

> *Everyday she sees you*
> *And she shivers inside.*
> *She sees that look on your face,*
> *That look in your eyes.*
> *Those few minutes you despised her,*
> *You didn't know who she was.*
> *You ground your teeth together*
> *And at this girl you swung.*
> *Who is she? Why is she here?*
> *Why does she anger me so?*
> *Why do I want to grab her neck*
> *And squeeze it till she chokes?*
> *I know that I am garbage,*
> *A bad excuse for a man,*
> *But maybe I'll feel better*
> *As her face hits my hand...*
> *Everyday I see you*
> *And I shake inside.*
> *That look you gave me is in my head,*

It makes me want to cry.
I'm angry, sad, upset, scared,
I don't know how to think.
I don't know when you'll come home
After having a few drinks.
I hate feeling this way
Because I need to be strong.
I have to keep telling myself
That you're the one who's wrong...
Everyday he sees her.
He knows he's done wrong.
And if he decides to do it again
She'll put him where he belongs.
Do whatever she needs.
She'll protect herself and the people she loves
And send you to hell for your deeds.
So try it.
I dare you.

—*Nicole Snyder*

Then there's the story of a heroin addict named Maurice who lectured kids about the dangers of heroin and other CNS depressants.

Maurice got into drugs at an early age to ease his suffering from low self-esteem. One day he shot up near an old-fashioned heat radiator in the apartment he was living in. He passed out with his face on it, and only woke up when his brother smelled his flesh burning and came and rescued him. Maurice was so numbed by the heroin he didn't even know he had seared off half his face. It took six or seven operations to make him presentable, but he was still disfigured and carried his scars with him as a reminder of the perils of heroin.

He used his appearance to reach some kids who wouldn't listen to anything else.

CHAPTER 10
Addiction to gambling

My son spends a lot of time on the Internet, and recently I've noticed I've got a lot of charges on my credit card that I can't explain. I think my son is at fault. What should I do?

ONE OF THE MOST INSIDIOUS PARTS OF THE INTERNET preys upon the low self-esteem of many of its users and not just by explicit sexual content. (That too is a symptom of low self-esteem, and we will address it in the next chapter.)

Gambling addicts are very closely related to alcoholics and drug addicts. Gamblers are looking for the same rush drug addicts feel, and the high they get from gambling helps to remove feelings of insecurity, inadequacy, or inferiority from which the gambler usually suffers. Like the alcoholic, the gambler may feel soothed or medicated by his gambling. In so many ways, the gambler is like other addicts, but perhaps it is all summed up best by the old saying that when men are shooting dice, the most scantily clad, beautiful woman in the world could walk by, and the gambler wouldn't see her. He has already been seduced by his gambling.

A gambling addict will experience the highs of many other stimulant drugs, but he or she will also end up in the lows, bottoming out like an alcoholic or cocaine addict. In the beginning, just the excitement of waiting for a game to start (particularly one upon which a bet has been made) is very similar to the cocaine addict who is exhilarated by the ritual or routine of copping his drugs, or from the alcoholic on his or her way to the bar. The common thread, always, is low self-esteem.

So in the beginning of the addiction, the gambler will experience the high of gambling, perhaps inflated by winnings, although not necessarily. Eventually, the gambler will experience low valleys as well. Sometimes this is brought on by a losing streak, which will certainly exacerbate the problem, but it doesn't necessarily cause it. For even if the gambler continues winning and winning, there is a hollow sense of victory. The gambling can never fill the hole the gambler feels inside; it takes more and more gambling to produce the desired tranquilizing or euphoric effects.

Meanwhile, the family of the gambler suffers many of the same degradations as the family of an alcoholic or a drug addict. The family will often have to "walk on eggshells" around the gambler. They wonder what type of mood the gambler will be in when he or she comes home. Did the gambler win or lose? Physical abuse may be a problem too. The gambler can also be gone for long stretches of time, leaving spouse and children alone and unhappy or frightened. The realization of this can feed the depression of the gambler, which drives the gambler even farther away from the family. Children who are gambling addicts experience these same problems, and we find that often, the parents do not understand the problems that motivate the child. It can be especially difficult to ferret out the gambling addict who is still an adolescent because his or her behavior is so similar to behavior brought on by other problems, as well as by normal teen angst.

The gambling addict, like the alcoholic or drug addict, will also take dangerous risks to support his habit. Like the alcoholic or addict, the gambler may lie, rob, steal, or even kill to get money to feed his addiction. But with the gambler the drug *is* the money. Some gamblers—even some teens—have resorted to bank robberies and other high-stakes misdeeds to support their habit. In the end it is usually the family that gets into financial trouble when the gambler blows all of his or her money and cannot meet minimum financial needs like paying bills and keeping the lights on.

Gamblers also may suffer from physical maladies because of their habit, much like their counterparts on drugs or alcohol or both. The gambler can suffer from heart problems because the addiction to gambling and the highly stressful environment brings about elevated blood pressure levels. These symptoms are amazingly similar to symptoms that alcoholics and drug addicts endure. This may be additional evidence of the lack of a magic bullet genetic predisposition to chemical abuse, for in the case of gambling, there are no chemicals whatsoever involved! Some drink or use other drugs but their primary addiction is gambling.

Yet the effects are very similar, and there are reasons for that. Surely, a gambler who gambles constantly *must*, by the very nature of the addiction, be able to understand when he or she has gone too far with gambling. After all, who would knowingly get on the phone to a bookie or walk up to a betting booth line and say, "I'd like to wager more money than I'm worth on this next game or race"?

But the language of gambling helps to insulate the gambler from that knowledge. It helps to insulate the gambler from the gambler's self-destructive behavior by obscuring the fact that a lot of money will change hands at the outcome of the next game or race. This is done by the way bets are placed. Serious gamblers do not often refer to the amount of money they are betting. They use the term "times." In the language of gambling, "times" equals five dollars. So, if a gambler calls up his bookie and says, "I want to go twenty times on the Super Bowl," he wants to bet $100 on the game. The language of gambling also assumes a percentage of the bet is paid to the bookie. This is also often not discussed and further enables the gambler to forget about the money involved. For example, in many cases a bookie will charge 10 percent on a bet. So, if you bet $100 on the Super Bowl at even odds and you won, you'd only get $100. If you lost, you'd have to pay $110.

As the odds get complicated and the bets more frequent, the "juice" that the bookie gets on a bet can add some spice to the gambler's life. He doesn't talk about how much he's betting, but tries to keep track of the odds and how much he has to pay out and how much he'll win. This can be very, very stimulating behavior. Add into it the fact that often the gambler is involved in illegal betting, and again you can see how very similar the addictive gambler is to the alcoholic and drug addict.

Other behaviors also parallel the alcoholic. Many of us have heard of the happy, sad, and mean drunk, and they all have their relatives in the gambler.

The "happy" gambler is the guy shooting dice. He's screaming, hollering, hand-slapping, giving high fives to other men and engaging in a male ritual that gives the gambler a lot of stimulation and excitement and takes him away from the stimuli or dynamics causing his low self-esteem. Also, by focusing on his obsessive behavior, i.e., the gambling, the gambler keeps himself from concentrating on the stimuli that have caused his low self-esteem.

The "sad" gambler is the gambler who is losing or has lost all of his money (like his weekly paycheck) but has figured out a way to pay his bills. He's sad because he lost, not necessarily because he lost the ability to pay his bills. If the "sad" gambler isn't careful he will end up like the "mean gambler."

The mean gambler is in despair and depression over the money he has lost and is having trouble figuring out how he's going to pay his bills. He is desperate and is probably manipulating friends and family to get money to fuel his addiction, and perhaps to pay his bills.

And then there is the Internet gambler. More insidious than the boy who throws dice on the street corner or bets the ponies, the Internet gambling addict may not even be recognized as such for many months or years. But a constant barrage of Internet e-mail advertising contributes to the gambling addict's behavior. Many of us have probably been solicited by the on-line gambling casinos or games of chance. Many of us may have even tried them once or twice. After all, they all advertise how easy the Internet makes gambling. "Do it from the comfort of your own home" is an actual quote from one of them. This is fine for the casual gambler, but a fatal attraction for the gambling addict. The Internet gambling addict usually has already spent much of his or her free time cruising the web, so gambling on-line is not an activity that will be instantly recognized.

Other warning signs also apply to all other types of gambling, many of which we've already discussed. But suffice it to say that a child running short of cash, who suddenly ends up watching ESPN to see who's going to win a ball game in a sport the child has never been interested in, involving two schools you've never heard of, is a possible candidate for a gambling addict and even an Internet gambler.

The Internet gambler, though, will probably not devote all of her gambling to on-line ventures. She is probably going to engage in more common gambling behavior too. All gamblers like to feel they're actually right in the game; it fuels a lot of different feelings, and betting on a game helps to make the gambler feel more in tune with the action. It may even help stimulate the high of competition that has been around since humankind first evolved. Granted the gambler is living vicariously through the efforts of others; still, the kid with $200 to $1,000 riding on the annual cutthroat college basketball game feels almost the same level of tension as the players in the game—some even more so. That is because if they don't have the money to pay the bookie, they are risking more than the players. Children in this situation can be nearly impossible to understand or handle at home. They can be so excitable that parents may think they've got a drunk or druggie on their hands. Rarely do they connect the dots and figure out what's really bothering their child.

While for many of us such games are a source of fun and may be community events experienced with friends, the gambler is only obsessed with the outcome and the rush of winning or crush of losing. That is all. They are the same as any other addict and experience the same highs and lows of any other form of addiction.

Let's take a look at a common gambling scenario. It is football
season and there a gambler is obsessively betting on football.
Beginning on Friday, usually, the gambler will place his bets for the
Saturday morning East Coast games. Now, by Saturday morning
he's looking at the afternoon games, usually without knowing how
he did in the morning. Many bookies will have a cut-off time around
noon or one o'clock East Coast time for the afternoon games. Come
the afternoon, the gambler will know the outcome of the morning
games and, good or bad, make his bets usually before four or five
o'clock East Coast time for the evening games. If the gambler is
behind, he may want to double or triple his usual bets, hoping to
play catch-up with the evening games. If the gambler is losing, he's
looking at the line his bookie is giving on any given game, the time
the game is played, the weather, who's hurt, and so on, trying to get
an edge on a game.

The next day is Sunday. Big day for the NFL, and the gambling
addict is again going through the same routine as he lines up his bets
during the day. He's looking at all the pro games, the times they
come on, the odds, the weather, and the rest. He's good and stimulated and very much into all of the action.

But now he's got a problem. What if come Monday morning he's
behind? Well, the bookie will likely let the gambler take one more
chance on the Monday Night Football game. It is a very big game
for gamblers, many of whom try to keep their gambling addiction
going "24-7" during football season. If the gambler loses on
Monday, the bookie will usually give the gambler a couple of days
to get the money together, so by Wednesday the gambler has settled
up. And guess what? There is often an NFL game on Thursday,
Friday is the beginning of betting for the college games, and so the
cycle continues—as long as the gambler has money.

Gamblers in this situation are so obsessed with the games that
even if they are around their family, they're not really there. More
than likely a gambler, if married and male, is going to have a foot-

ball widow for a wife. That gambler is going to be far more focused on the betting and the games than he is on his wife or children—especially if he's losing. Fear is a big stimulus and a big motivator.

That's what it's all about. The gambler is getting stimulation from the betting, the possible losing, owing money, being yelled at, watching the games…All of the behavior feeds, stimulates, and medicates the low self-esteem monster inside the gambler. But the bottom line is obvious: the bookie doesn't care.

Reality then comes crashing in on the gambler when he tries to explain not having the money for the bookie. "I don't want a story, I want money," is the bookie's universal cry and he doesn't care how the gambler gets the money. This is where the phone calls begin. Harassing telephone calls can lead to personal visits as the bookie continues to press for collection.

In the movie *Parenthood*, Tom Hulce, playing the gambling-addicted son of Jason Robards, is thrown from a moving car by a bookie trying to collect a debt. Hulce tries to play it off as merely a bunch of friends to his father, who has seen it take place. "Friends?" his father says. "Friends slow down…."

Such activity can occur, but the bookmaker usually doesn't want to hurt anybody. He just wants his money and he'll sometimes give gamblers a certain amount of time to come up with the money before getting tough himself or selling the bad debt to a loan shark for 35 to 50 percent of the money owed. Gambling addicts will often get in further trouble here as they try to find a different bookie to lay their bets off on. The gambler will try to make enough money from the second bookie to pay off the first. Robbing Peter to pay Paul, though, rarely works, and soon the gambling addict will find himself in debt to two, three, perhaps as many as five different bookies.

This is when things can get desperate for gamblers. They're obsessed with gambling, which is the only way they can alleviate their uncomfortable thoughts. But now the gambling is an uncomfortable thought. The deeper in debt, the more people are after them, the more depressed they become and the more desperate. The more they gamble to forget, the more they need to make the big score to get out of the hole.

Paul was such a case. He grew up in a very abusive family. His father was physically abusive and never spent a lot of time with him. Paul was introduced to gambling early in life and in adolescence started to play cards, pool, and dice for money. He moved into betting sports by his teen years. Paul ended up in debt to a bookie for several thousand dollars. Desperate, and not particularly bright, Paul decided to rob a bank. He thought he had an angle; he didn't have the nerve to draw a gun on someone, so he bought a monkey—yes, a monkey.

The idea was to train the monkey to take bags from people so that Paul, by slipping the monkey through the night deposit box after hours, could somehow take bags of money from the bank. But instead, Paul was caught with the monkey at the bank, whereupon he was quickly, and probably hilariously, arrested. He ended up in therapy and started attending Gamblers Anonymous meetings. He has now lived several years without gambling.

Remember too that the forbidden is very stimulating. As a child, if your mother told you not to touch the cookie jar, what was the first thing you wanted to do? You wanted to put your hands right in the cookie jar. That "cookie jar" syndrome is prevalent with many addicts and those with low self-esteem. Something of an adrenaline rush is experienced when doing the socially unacceptable, the risky, or perhaps even the illegal. So it is with sports betting. The whole idea of dealing with somebody in the underworld who may be a member of organized crime is especially exciting for the gambling addict—until the gambler gets in over his head.

In the popular television drama *The Sopranos*, Tony Soprano speaks of a "degenerate gambler." The reason Tony allowed the man to continue to bet with him was because Tony knew the gambler owned a business and would one day gamble it all away. It was a sad commentary about gambling addicts and true to life about what can happen to them. The seduction of gambling preys upon the weakness of the gambler—and not just by the Tony Sopranos of the world.

Casinos seduce the gambler with fine rooms, comp tickets, free meals, boxing matches, entertainment, and cheap and plentiful alcohol. Just as the drug dealer seduces his clients, so does the casino.

Notice that alcohol and other drugs can be part of the experience, for the gambling addict who's losing voluminous amounts of cash may self-medicate with alcohol, cocaine, marijuana, or other drugs. This invites dual addictions, which we often see in treating gamblers. We also see a great difference between the male and the female gambling addict. Male addicts usually started gambling at a young age, whereas most women don't start until adulthood, usually spurred on by a traumatic event.

It is particularly difficult to spot a gambling addict. They are not going to show a lot of physical symptoms like someone addicted to drugs. Their eyes won't be dilated and their clothes won't smell of marijuana or alcohol. *The only way to uncover a gambling addict is to follow the money.*

Money is the medium used to gamble, and once someone becomes a serious gambler, the need for cash will make itself known in many ways. The gambler may not even realize this, which is why gambling can be a worse addiction than even heroin. With drugs the users eventually might become aware that if they continue with their addiction they will die. Not so with most gamblers. They have no physical symptoms, so they continue gambling, because there is always the possibility that they can make the "big score."

There is an abundance of clichés to cover the phenomenon of compulsive gambling. One is "If you go slow, you gotta go," or the opposite, "If you go fast, you can't last." Either way, as both sayings show, the odds are against you and eventually you're going to end up broke and in despair. This is epitomized in the other cliché, "I live to gamble and gamble to live." Follow that cliché up with the other oldie, "The day you lay off is the day it'll pay off," and you see how and why gamblers continue to pour their time, money, and other resources into their addiction.

Again, ritualistic behavior comes into play. A gambler betting the ponies is the first one at the track. He's in the paddock, the stables, talking to horse trainers, assessing the weights of the jockey, the horse, and everyone's past performance. He'll look to see where the horse is situated at the starting gate. He'll get his rush fantasizing and plotting ways to make money on the bet. Like a heroin addict, he's eager to score and all the ritualistic window dressing of the event spurs him on more.

Many times these gamblers have no nurturing father figure in their lives and, like the drug addict, they couldn't care less about their appearance as long as they have enough money to gamble. Once in recovery these gamblers have an especially hard time adjusting.

It may take them years to give up gambling, and they will often fall back. The first sign of this could be the "mind bet," whereby the gambler will watch games and pretend to gamble on his favorite teams. Which brings to mind one of the best clichés from Gamblers Anonymous: "Don't make a mind bet. You may lose your mind."

Finally, on the subject of the mind and its intricacies, a recent *Newsweek* article pointed out that, when gamblers get the rush of gambling, they have feelings similar to what a cocaine addict gets upon using cocaine. In fact the same brain centers are stimulated. Which once again goes to show that there is really only one addiction, but many forms of it, and gambling is as serious an addiction as alcohol or heroin, although many people do not grasp that as yet.

CHAPTER 11
Addiction to other people

"My daughter is always clinging to me and can't seem to make a decision without tacit approval from either me or my husband. Is this normal?"

CHILDREN WHO ARE ADDICTED TO OTHER PEOPLE are not only suffering from low self-esteem, but to get any sense of self-worth only from other people. These children become people-pleasers and often do whatever it takes to gain acceptance from others. They are co-dependent. Co-dependents are usually defined as people who depend on someone else to make them feel good or give them a sense of worth.

Co-dependents can be very needy. They can also have a need to be needed, because this gives them a sense of control, a sense of power. The power in turn feeds their low self-worth and enables them to feel better about themselves. According to statistics from Co-Dependents Anonymous, there are ninety million co-dependents in the United States. Many came from alcoholic families, but certainly all came from some dysfunctional setting that made them believe they needed to please others in order to be accepted. And that if they weren't accepted, they had no value.

Both men and women suffer from this symptom of low self-esteem, but we treat many more women than men in this area. Women are taught to fill the needs of others, to be selfless. Many religions preach this as a virtue. But such a virtue can become a vice when the *only* way a person can feel good is by making *others* feel good, especially at the expense of herself. True, many religions also teach selfless sacrifice, and who among us wouldn't give our own life for the lives of our children? But the co-dependent crosses over to self-destructive behavior, usually for no particular reason, for the sake of others, who are suffering from low self-esteem themselves.

A child of low self-esteem finds gratification in doing for others. Take Tommy, for example, a gifted basketball player who wanted the friendship of a child named Paul. Tommy was gifted, but he was new to the area and Paul was the child everyone perceived to be the "cool kid" at Tommy's middle school. Naturally Paul had to challenge Tommy to a game of one-on-one basketball and naturally Tommy won handily. But soon Tommy found that if he let Paul win, then Paul would be his friend. Tommy became a people-pleaser and used this power to obtain friendship.

A child like Tommy who learns such a lesson will find it very gratifying to be counted on and very pleasing to be the center of attention and to have control over a situation.

Because the child fears rejection or abandonment, helping other people keeps those twin wolves at bay. Early on, children can come to feel different from others, less than others, estranged from their peers, or feel they don't fit in at home. Perhaps a chance event of helping someone at school, or doing something at home that brings an unexpected accolade will spark their desire to please. The risk is that behavior detrimental to these children will be praised and reinforced, causing all kinds of problems.

You've seen it and heard of it a million times—"falling in with the wrong crowd" and "kissing up." We have found that many of our clients who come in for drug or alcohol rehabilitation also have tendencies toward co-dependence. Enabling parents are often to blame for the child's ultimate low self-esteem. In many of these cases the mother will be very dependent on the child and the child becomes an extension of the mother, or perhaps the father. The parent will try to get gratification out of the child needing her; in these situations, with this type of co-dependent, this enabling parent will do whatever necessary to take care of and enable that child.

As a result, the child may never learn to have any self-respect or confidence in his own abilities because he's gone through few trials and tribulations in life. The co-dependent mother, for example, is always there to get the child out of trouble, or to explain away aberrant behavior.

Some co-dependent parents also sabotage their children so they can constantly be there to take care of them. Some parents will act out when they see their children in recovery. Sometimes they set their child up to fail and then, when the child fails, the parents step in and help again. Usually this is done almost unconsciously—the parents are seldom aware of their own behavior.

When coaching these parents on their behavior, we have had some success teaching them the do's and don'ts of how to help a child headed toward addiction. These parents change their behavior, cutting the umbilical cord, as it were, and by doing so give their child a chance to make his or her own decisions. We teach the parents to let the child become his own person while at the same time instilling the discipline the child also needs. It is a fine line to walk, especially with parents who have co-dependent children. It is also difficult because many such parents thrive on the attention and gratification they get from having their child constantly in need of them.

But it is difficult. A co-dependent parent is constantly concerned with the "what ifs" of healing. What if my child no longer needs me? What if my child gets well? These parents don't want an independent child. That would mean the needy parent would be out of a job, struggling to find a new way to feed his need for improving his own self-worth. This is rarely, of course, a conscious thought.

Meanwhile, the child may become involved with other people and become addicted to them by being a people-pleaser—doing the same thing to others as they do to their parents. And, of course, without the stringent guidelines inherent in a parent and child relationship, a people-pleasing child can become a very dangerous child indeed. They will go to extremes such as stealing money to treat their friends, or to shower their friends with gifts. They will show unbelievable support for their friends, support that should be of a suspicious nature in and of itself.

The friend who calls to see if you are all right after a nasty fall is one thing. The friend who calls ten or twelve times a day, visits twice, brings gifts, and so on, is another. This may show that someone is as addicted to other people as some are to heroin.

It is extremely important to find out what causes this obsessive need for people early on. Low self-esteem, again, is like a cancer, and it can only worsen. A female who is obsessed with others may migrate toward someone who is an alcoholic or drug addict simply from the need to be needed. "I can change him. I can help him," may be her cry. Day-to-day needs may be dropped or forgotten as one addict (the people addict) takes care of the other (the drug or alcohol addict).

It is not unusual for resentment to build as the people addict cares for the drug addict or alcoholic almost exclusively. Fights can occur. The people-addicted co-dependent can get stuck paying bills, registering cars, putting food on the table, and the rest. Many of these relationships can be doomed, but even so the people addict, though carrying around a lot of resentment, will get gratification and even power and control by being the "go to" person in the relationship.

Again, education and treatment are the only things that can help these individuals. Support groups for alcoholics and drug and gambling addicts can also help people addicts. It is often essential for co-dependents to get involved in such groups, if for no other reason than to become aware of their own addictive behavior. Those who are addicted to people are usually very slow in recognizing their addiction and even slower in doing anything about it. After all, we all want to care for each other, we all value those who help out others, and we all want to believe that we are doing right in helping others. That such behavior, taken to extremes, can be debilitating or may have its roots in low self-esteem is something many of us never fully realize.

We had one patient named Mark who is an example of this problem. Mark came to us when he was fifteen. He had been caught on a drug screen at school and admitted to a drug problem. Mark's mother wanted him in treatment as soon as possible. Mark's mother was a single parent—the father had abandoned them early on (another example of problems caused by the same-gender parent). Mark hardly knew his father.

In the beginning there was an insurance problem and Mark's mother got on the phone and argued for hours with her managed care company in order to get her son into treatment. She was blunt and outspoken. She made sure everyone knew how hard she was fighting to get Mark help. Finally, she succeeded. Mark came into treatment and we hooked him up with a male therapist to get the male nurturing he wasn't getting with his father and he started to do very well.

But when the mother came into sessions with us she would talk about how bad Mark was and how he did everything wrong. She seemed incapable of giving Mark any positive feedback for the efforts he'd taken or the progress he'd made since his treatment had begun. Meanwhile, Mark continued in our program, and after a month his urine tests were clean.

That's when we had to evaluate the mother.

We advised her to do the following:
1. Explain your feelings and anger, but stop criticizing and demeaning your child.
2. Set specific consequences for negative or self-destructive behavior and follow through on them.
3. Let your child know when he does something good. Everyone needs a pat on the back.
4. Recognize that life is not all positive or all negative. It is a combination of both.

5. Never reward negative behavior. People will not
change negative behavior if it is rewarded.

Still, the mother seemed incapable of giving Mark any positive
feedback whatsoever. She continued to focus on how bad he was
and not on what he was achieving. Mark, of course, picked up on
his mother's continued displeasure, and thus her criticisms became a
self-fulfilling prophecy. Soon Mark began to slip, and after sixteen
weeks in our program, he again showed signs of drug addiction. All
of his good work was sabotaged by his mother.

The problem was compounded by the managed care company
that cut down on his sessions. But Mark's mother didn't fight the
company for her son because we had called her on the carpet for her
style of parenting. So, before long, Mark left the program and was
arrested for stealing a car while under the influence of alcohol.

The mother was right there to help, right away. She called and
demanded that we get Mark back into treatment. She argued with
her managed care company to get Mark back to us. But, at the
same time, she refused to come in for help herself. She didn't see
how illogical she was in dealing with her son. First she wanted him
to get better, then she seemingly did not. She fought with her managed care company, then didn't, and then did again. Nothing she
did seemed to follow any sense of purpose—on the surface. All her
son saw was a mother who constantly demeaned him and then
bailed him out.

Mark stayed with us a short time, the second time around, and
then went back to his mother. A short time later he was arrested
again for stealing a car. His mother was the first one down at the
court house screaming at the injustice, screaming at the judge and
the cops, telling them how wrong they were. But she still told her
son what a worthless person he was.

By this time, of course, Mark was suffering from a very low self-
esteem problem and his mother's actions were quickly pushing him

toward more drugs and depression. He acted out against his mother, who told him how bad he was and that reinforced his low self-image. Bear in mind that the more trouble he got into, the more he needed to be rescued and therefore the more he needed his mother. This in turned fueled her need to be needed. So she continued to have power and control over the child by reminding him how worthless he was.

After the second arrest we got to see Mark for a third time. We saw the same pattern of behavior from his mother. Once again she fought with the authorities, fought with us, fought for Mark, and then fought against him. It was exasperating. We felt we couldn't do any more work with his mother, but held out hopes of helping Mark. Our game plan was to put Mark into an in-patient program, an extended program in a hospital that would be followed by a stay at a half-way house. Both arenas would allow us to get Mark the intensive counseling we thought would be successful (based on the limited earlier success we had with him) while giving him a break from his mother. By this time Mark was nearly eighteen and we hoped that by separating him from his mother for a short period we could help him to help himself, become independent, and bolster his self-esteem. We hoped he would gain some sense of self-respect and eventually could continue his relationship with his mother but on a more healthy footing.

It must be said here that our goal was not to separate a child from his mother; rather it was to help both of them build a healthy, mature relationship. We were partially successful. Mark got away from his mother for a time and has been sober now for years. He also gained insight into his mother's co-dependence. As it turns out, the mother grew up in an alcoholic family herself and had been constantly criticized as a child. She then fed it back to her own son without being fully aware of what she was doing.

When Mark figured out why his mother was the way she was, he figured out why he had turned out the way he had. His drug use and addiction, even his stealing cars, were all attempts to bolster his self-esteem.

Mark got well. But we didn't have as much luck with his mother. To this day she is still as critical as ever and Mark reports she still tries to keep him dependent on her. For example, shortly after he left the half-way house Mark went home for the Christmas holiday. (We had, of course, coached his mother on the way to support her son's recovery.) But he hadn't been home more than a few minutes when she offered him a glass of wine, knowing full well that as a recovering addict he was not supposed to have any mind-altering substances.

Parents do not normally pick their newborn babies up at the hospital thinking, "Boy, I wonder how I can screw this kid's life up." It isn't that at all. No parent wants to be viewed as a bad parent. Most parents merely want the best for their children, as Mark's mother often claimed she did. The problem is that many parents have learned behaviors that were passed on by their parents, which were passed on by their parents, ad infinitum, and they just don't have the skills or knowledge to help their children. Often the parents aren't even aware of their deficiencies and can become defensive when approached about them. This is particularly true of the parents who were children of parents suffering from low self-esteem and addiction.

Another case pertaining to this point is a young girl, Susan, who came to us for counseling after she was stopped in a car with other teens and police found marijuana under the seat of the car. Sue underwent an evaluation and the test came back positive, not only for marijuana but for heroin as well. Sue grew up in an alcoholic family with a father who criticized and demeaned her. Usually he wasn't around, but constantly working. Susan believed her father didn't care about her because the few times they did interact, he spent the time criticizing her. Compounding the problem was the fact that Susan's father was a bit of a perfectionist. This ultimately, as so often happens in similar circumstances between father and daughter, turned Susan into a people-pleaser.

She also became addicted to young men because she was obsessed with male nurturing. That's when she ran into Billy. Billy had a problem with marijuana and heroin, and Susan, who was an honor roll student and a concert violinist, turned her back on her academic and musical pursuits to please him. She felt as long as she had Billy and pleased him she had some worth. The male nurturing she received from him felt good to her. He, meanwhile, became more and more strung out on heroin. This fueled her needs as well, because it gave her a certain amount of power and control over Billy. He certainly wasn't going to leave her.

To make sure, she began using heroin as well, not only to give them more of a common bond, but to make sure she didn't lose Billy to another junkie. Susan became strung out, got worse, flunked out of school, and gave up any hope of a future by moving in with Billy. She took a hostess and waitress job to earn money to keep them in their small apartment and supply their growing drug habits.

Eventually, at the ripe old age of twenty, Billy became infected with hepatitis C. Finally, because of the hepatitis, Bill had to check into a hospital, where he received treatment and was eventually graduated into a rehab facility. Susan, as most could predict by now, tried to get herself checked into the same facility.

We separated them.

Billy soared in rehab, becoming more independent and more confident, but Susan became uncomfortable. She'd lost power and control over Billy—the things that fed her need for acceptance. She was suffering not only heroin withdrawal, but Billy withdrawal. Eventually Billy left Susan and she became extremely depressed. When she lost that final element of control, at nineteen years of age, Susan snapped, and attempted suicide by slashing her wrists.

Luckily we got Susan into a hospital, stabilized, and eventually into more intensive therapy. While there Susan became aware of her destructive tendencies and came to realize she did not love Billy and never had. This story ended happily as Susan continued in recovery, ended up going to college, playing the violin, and after graduation went on to a stunning career teaching and performing music.

But Susan had to overcome the need to be needed and all the other needs that her abusive father never fulfilled. More to the point, she had to learn to pursue those needs in a healthy manner, instead of a self-destructive one. *Getting over the fear of abandonment* is critical when we treat these cases. Usually this fear is associated with most co-dependence cases. It is a fuel that feeds the addiction to other people. This fear of abandonment can come from physical abandonment or may be caused by rejection, criticism, abuse, neglect, or apathy.

A final case shows that even in the most extreme cases of co-dependence, there is still cause for hope, even if the co-dependence is not caught until adulthood. Jeannie met Darren when both of them were in their early twenties. They eventually became close and Jeannie felt Darren was the man that would "make me whole." She became extremely addicted to him and even when Darren became abusive, she stayed with the relationship.

Many police officers who answer domestic disturbance calls will tell you that those and traffic stops are the most dangerous. The reason domestic disturbances can be dangerous is that while women who are being battered may call the police, once the police arrive, they will turn and defend the man abusing them, sometimes starting life-threatening fights with the police officers. It is a desperate cry for control.

Such was the case with Jeannie. The police were called, complaints filed, but then Jeannie would turn around and sabotage the complaint or claim that the physical abuse had not occurred. She stayed and defended Darren to police, judges, and all comers, despite the fact she was receiving brutal and frequent beatings.

Darren, on top of his brutal temper, or in conjunction with it, developed quite a crack habit. He tried to cajole and romance

Jeannie between beatings, claiming it would never happen again. As is often the case, Jeannie believed him and stuck by him. But Darren's behavior got more and more erratic as he smoked more and more crack, and he became increasingly paranoid and delusional.

It got to the point that he began suffering from cocaine psychosis. He would return home and accuse Jeannie of all kinds of strange things. He once accused her of having sex with three elves or midgets and he claimed that when he entered the room the midgets/elves would run to the ceiling and crawl through the vents in the ceiling. On that occasion when Jeannie denied having a wild sexual adventure with a group of midgets/elves, Darren severely beat her. She arrived in therapy with bruises and a black eye still defending Darren!

But, as it turns out, that event did change things. Jeannie, who had extended forays away from reality, was not so gone that she could believe in Darren after the midget/elf episode. Eventually Jeannie decided she had all she could take and began to get some co-dependence counseling. At that time Jeannie developed a clear understanding of why she had a need for Darren and why it was unhealthy. She too had been abandoned by her father at an early age, which set her up to become male dependent.

We used the fact that she had recently had a child to get her to understand that a baby living in violent conditions was very vulnerable to all kinds of emotional problems. It was only her understanding that her baby could be in danger from Darren's wrath that convinced Jeannie in the beginning to break away from him. However, after being in therapy for a while, she gained confidence in herself and some self-respect. She went to secretarial school while working as many jobs as possible, then went to work for a major pharmaceutical company.

Darren wasn't so fortunate. He continued to abuse cocaine and became so psychotic that he wound up in a state psychiatric hospital for the insane.

This and our other cases show that in many cases of low self-esteem we have to deal with a variety of addictions. But remember, there is still only one source. Our goal is to try and reach out to the people and discover what is the root cause of their low self-esteem and to treat the various symptoms they display. *In the case of co-dependents we are always dealing with an unhealthy need to be needed.* Through this activity the co-dependent person looks to obtain a real sense of security, power, and control. Through those methods they may obtain a false self-esteem. But in the end, we teach these co-dependents that self-esteem must come from within, not from without.

Young children have a natural tendency to please. Children, looking up to their parents, wish to please them. It makes us all feel good to be wanted and smiled at by those we love. But if the parent is unhealthy, then the child may become pathologically addicted to the need to please others. Their lives can be in disarray. They feel abandoned. They want and they need. The child, if not addressed by the parent, will feel out of control. They begin to try anything to please their parents and others.

This brings control. It brings a sense of relief. It has to be channeled and recognized for what it is before the child graduates to the point where she's being beaten in her early twenties for having imaginary flings with elves.

PART III
THE CURE, AND BUILDING SELF-ESTEEM

CHAPTER 12
The intervention

"I want to do something about my child's low self-esteem and addiction, but I've heard that something as direct as an intervention isn't the best. What should I do?"

THERE IS AN OLD SAYING THAT THERE IS NO SUCH THING as a bad intervention and, up to a point, we readily agree with that statement. The sooner parents intervene in a case where their child is suffering from low self-esteem, the better. It is much easier to turn around a twelve-year-old or even a fifteen-year-old than it is to get to a seventeen- or eighteen-year-old. It isn't that a younger child is more easily influenced by adults. It isn't that they are more cooperative or communicative, or their problems less serious. Our studies have shown that children as young as eleven or twelve have entertained thoughts of suicide.

But, at an earlier age, the low self-esteem has not entrenched itself in the child's psyche as deeply as it has in an older teen through patterns of a behavior detrimental to the existence of the organism. Simply stated, the younger the child, the easier it is to regain control and guide him because the parent has much more leverage over a younger than an older child.

Most children who end up committing suicide are older, but the low self-esteem and depression have already manifested themselves before the child reaches his or her teen years and that's when parents have to intervene. If at all possible the parents or the guardian of the child should initiate the first intervention and, to do that, they must recognize the warning signs of low self-esteem. Once identified, the parents should confront the child immediately and jointly. If there is but one parent in the family, the parent may choose to proceed alone, or in consort with a close friend or family member or professional for added support. However, be prepared to be lambasted by your child during and after the intervention.

For those parents who question whether they should intervene, we urge them to remember they have a moral obligation to intervene in their children's lives. For those unimpressed by moral obligations, please consider this: parents are legally obligated to their children until the children are adults—an age that varies from state to state. If you are nervous about a possible intervention, please consult professional caregivers where you live for advice and assistance in the matter.

Clinically, why it is important to intervene at an early age with children is a little more complex than either the moral or legal considerations, but it is essential to understand when trying to render assistance. When children are very young they derive most of their self-esteem from how they are treated by their parents. A young child who is told he is ugly, or stupid, or a "bad seed" will endeavor to act in such a manner. They come to believe they are what they are called and told by their parents. This is not to say that parents should inflate children's egos and tell them they are constantly the best, the brightest, and the cutest, but it is to say parents should seek ways to discipline while at the same time giving their children something to be proud of, or something in which they can excel. Parents must help children find their niche, or their special God-given talents. The more time parents put into the child, the more they are going to get out of that child, and the more solid foundation they will build for the child's self-esteem.

So it can be said that a parental intervention is not a one-time affair, but rather an on-going process. Parents must be involved with their children and come to realize that each step they take in guiding, assisting, and disciplining their children is actually an intervention of sorts. Intervening early is key to keeping children from traveling down the road to low self-esteem. It is sometimes compared to cancer treatment. Just as the earlier you detect and remove a cancer the better your chances are of recovery, so it is with low self-esteem.

Utilizing the warning signs we've talked about in this book, and looking for evidence of certain addictions, parents must remain vigilant and ready to intervene at a moment's notice. Remember the investment you have in your children and be ready to confront them if necessary, speak to them when warranted, and spend as much time as needed to assist them. It is a shame to hear or watch parents who will spend so much time on their careers, their cars, or fixing up their home, but have no time for their children. We've gone over the different types of parenting problems that can cause this, but here let's concentrate on how any parent can conduct an intervention.

TAKING THE FIRST STEP. Parents need to take a deep breath and think. Before any direct action takes place the parents must try to understand what bothers their child or what is motivating their child. Knowing what is specifically wrong with a child prepares parents to deal with the motivation behind acts brought on by low self-esteem, because most negative actions come from the root cause of low self-esteem. Scratch a bully and you'll find a child deeply insecure or a child who feels inadequate. The meanest, the most seemingly evil child will have, at the heart of it, a feeling he is unworthy; he will be depressed and riddled with angst. Once the parent understands this, taking the next step will be much easier.

THE SECOND STEP. The way psychotherapy works is not magic. In fact, psychotherapy has been called a mental dump. That's exactly the truth. In psychotherapy we assist people to get out their negative feelings by turning those feelings into language. This occurs in a majority of our cases. So if a child feels safe and secure with his parents, who better to act as a therapist? Who has a closer connection, greater rapport, closer bond than the child's own parents? No one.

So parents must set aside some time to conduct their intervention. Find a time good for both the parent and the child, but insist that enough time be taken to talk. Then open up the dialogue and prod the child to discuss her problems. If the parents intervene early on and allow the child to share her negative feelings in a safe place where she feels she won't be belittled or criticized or physically abused, then the child will dump a lot of the negative angst she's been carrying around.

Parents should also take this opportunity to share with their child what they perceive as problems—conditions a child may have over-looked. It should also be presented in a manner that enhances a child's understanding of the problem. So, instead of saying, "Son, you idiot, you don't go skateboarding without wearing knee pads," perhaps the parent can offer, "Son, hey, I'm forty and you're twelve. Let me offer you some advice, no knee pads equals blood and pain. I'm telling you this because I love you."

It is better not to put the child down with an insult, but present him with a new idea he can embrace. But, in the end, the parent can also say, "Son, I'm forty and you're twelve. I'm morally and legally responsible for you. We will do it my way."

THE THIRD STEP. As the Boy Scouts say, "Be prepared." Confrontation, however mildly enacted, can lead to volatile arguments and, in some cases, physical altercations. Cut down the odds by being willing to listen and explain your points firmly but quietly. Whatever else happens during an intervention, do not lose your temper. Also, it is wise to bring friends and family members along. In one intervention we knew of, a brother confronted his sister about her alcoholism. This occurred after the brother, we'll call him Tommy, found his sister Susan drinking alone at home with her children in the middle of the day and trying to light a fire in her fireplace with wood she'd pried from her backyard deck.

"You think that I'm weak," Susan told her brother.

"No. Alcoholism isn't a character flaw," her brother explained. "It is a disease. If you had seven of the ten warning signs for cancer, wouldn't you want me to tell you? It's the same with alcohol."

Tommy intervened while taking a walk with his sister and their other brother through her neighborhood. It took several interventions before she finally agreed to seek therapy. This brings up another point; there's no such thing as a "model" or "ideal" intervention. You must know your subject, and if the person who is to benefit from the intervention is apt to feel "ganged up on" by having a host of people confronting him or her, then perhaps you should consider a smaller intervention wherein the subject will feel more comfortable and therefore more receptive. Always remember the important phrase "I care" during these interventions. Let the subject of the intervention know that the reason for the intervention is because you care about them. It's not from spite, and therefore not from anger, but from love. This will be the seed to understanding, and it can disarm the child during the intervention.

Sometimes a large confrontation is what is necessary, and sometimes you may want to intervene with the help of a clinician or a doctor. You must be prepared by doing your homework before the intervention.

An extreme example is if you intend to intervene on a distraught loved one known to possess and use firearms. Another example of this is if you are a single mother and intend to run an intervention on your teen-age son who outweighs you by thirty pounds. In both cases a little bit of advanced planning can lessen the chances of a volatile and dangerous situation later. It is often preferable, when planning to intervene, to consult with a care provider who has trained for and participated in interventions. It cannot be understated how much advanced planning is necessary in an initial intervention.

Go through a list of people you would invite. Consider the mindset of the person who will benefit from the intervention and find a way to confront him in a setting that you choose and that will minimize the potential for drama. In Tommy's case with Susan, he chose to take a walk with her in her neighborhood, knowing she would not want to create a scene there.

Finally, be prepared to bring in professional help as well as for some surprises when you intervene.

This brings us to Patrick. Patrick came to see us when he was fifteen years old. He was trouble. He'd been expelled from high school. Teachers had said Patrick's defiant attitude made it nearly impossible to deal with him. Complicating the issue was Patrick's slight learning disability and the beginnings of alcoholism.

Patrick's mother became concerned, recognized the early warning signs of alcoholism, and intervened. It was this intervention that ultimately brought about a solution to a problem she hadn't foreseen. For her, it was all about stepping in and putting a stop to the abuse of alcohol.

When Patrick admitted his problem at home, his mother brought him to us for an initial evaluation. Here is where the intervention had unforeseen consequences, for at our initial evaluation we came to the conclusion that Patrick's father wasn't around very much, so we assigned a male therapist to Patrick to help the boy get some much needed male nurturing. It was then we found out how deeply Patrick missed and needed his father.

He told us he felt unimportant and was convinced his father didn't love him. He told us about his dad having to work, and that there was something wrong with him because his father had to work often. Patrick also expressed feelings of low worth and inferiority. During a six-month period, working with a male therapist, Patrick's attitude about himself began to change. He smiled more and felt more confident about himself.

At that point we tried to bring his father back into the picture and have him attend a session with Patrick. It didn't work because the father said he was tied down with work, including a major bonus for performance. We tried to explain how important it was for him to spend time with Patrick, but it didn't make much of an impression. He remained convinced that Patrick's problems were minor and could be easily solved.

Patrick's father didn't realize that it is best to intervene early, nor did he come to realize that an intervention was necessary. He was wrapped up in his own world where he thought he was doing the best thing possible for his family, not realizing that having an expensive roof over his head and every possible electronic gadget was not what the child needed.

So we tried another approach and told the father that if he didn't spend time with his son now, he was going to have to spend money down the road on a lot of attorney's fees and therapy. The father dismissed that idea and said he thought his son was doing much better.

About a year later, Patrick stole the family car, got drunk with a group of his friends, wrecked the car, and ended up with several stitches in his head.

Immediately, Patrick came back to us, and we asked his parents if they had been following our recommendations. The mother said no, they had not, and took us aside to tell us that although they had plenty of money, her husband, Patrick's father, seemed obsessed with making money, spending almost no time with his son. We began treatment again, and again tried to get the father more involved in Patrick's life, but to no avail.

Therapy wasn't as easy the second time around either. Patrick was more belligerent and defiant and more into the drug culture. The father refused to believe there was anything wrong with his son. He perceived the boy to be "high-spirited" but not dangerous. Consequently, Patrick faced no consequences for his recalcitrant behavior.

Two months later, while Patrick was still in treatment, he got picked up by the police for again stealing the family car. This time he was busted with several ounces of marijuana in the car. The guy riding with him turned out to be a drug dealer. As it happened, they were busted near a school, which complicated the legal matters in

New Jersey. And the dealer wouldn't claim responsibility for the drugs found in the car. This time, an attorney wanted $5,000 to $6,000 up front before he would represent Patrick.

Meanwhile, we responded by getting the boy more into intensive therapy at a rehab and once again tried to get the father involved, at any level, with his son. The father still resisted and said he was too busy with work to get involved in family counseling. Everything the boy did screamed for his father to get involved in his life, but the father wouldn't do it—at least not at any appreciable level. Mind you, the father continued to believe he *was* involved with his son by working hard and making money for the family. We finally got the father involved in therapy, but only when Patrick was facing possible jail time. At that point it became apparent to the father that the best way to help his son was to make the time to attend counseling sessions. It kept Patrick out of jail and helped clear up the problems within the family.

In counseling it came out that Patrick's father was obsessed with making money because he had grown up poor and in very squalid conditions. He had grown to adulthood with a fear that he would one day again be poor and that drove him to try harder and harder to make money. Once we helped him to see that he didn't have to be so obsessed with money, he began to ease back on the work load and spend more time with his son, who ended up sober, clean, and in college.

Patrick's story is not unique. Many parents do what his father did. They'll parent according to the trauma they've suffered as children. That learned behavior from the trauma isn't very healthy, and we have to ferret it out and discuss it. This will help parents get involved in the life of their children, which in turn will help keep the children from low self-esteem, depression, and abuse.

As we've often said, parents must pay attention to their child's activities and be aware of their child's behaviors. Take, for example, self-mutilation. Some children will obsessively scratch themselves, or twirl and pull out their own hair. Some have mutilated themselves so badly that they are riddled with scars and scratches, or are so obsessive about hair pulling that they leave big bald patches on their head, or pluck out all their eyebrows.

These activities can also be the result of low self-esteem; the child is trying to get away from his or her uncomfortable feelings through self-mutilation. One such girl I met early in my career told me when I visited her in the hospital that she liked to cut herself to feel numb. She usually used razor blades, and she said that when she felt her warm blood dripping down her arms and her legs it gave her a feeling of numbness and soothed her. It got rid of the toxic feelings she was carrying inside. The more she cut herself, the more she focused on the act and the more it took her out of her tormenting reality and away from the angst of everyday life.

Finally, let's take a look at a very informative case in which the parent was right on top of things. Her name was Mary and her daughter Martha was the problem. Martha was raised by her mother and a stepfather after her biological father abandoned her. Martha got a lot of nurturing from her mother and her stepfather and she seemed to be doing very well. She was an honor roll student, never caused the parents any problems, and seemed to be the perfect daughter.

But, one morning Mary noticed that her daughter had a spot of blood on one of her socks. It was just one time. One incident. One stray look by the mother. But it portended some radical events in Mary and Martha's life. The daughter, all of sixteen, quickly confessed that she was obsessively scratching herself, but didn't seem to know why.

Mary then gave us a call and brought her daughter in for an evaluation. Quickly we came to learn that Martha blamed herself for her father's absence in her life. She felt defective and inferior. And while doing great in school and great at home, she was entertaining suicidal thoughts. She didn't have a plan figured out, but she was well on the path to self-destruction. Typically, she told us, she could only gain relief from excessively scratching her leg.

In therapy a lot of her feelings came out. We engaged in role play-ing, and during those times when I would pretend to be her, and she would pretend to be the therapist, she came to understand that she felt responsible for her parents' breakup and her father's abandon-ment, and finally came to realize how she had been wrong in think-ing that way.

Martha got help and got a lot better, but only because her mother intervened the moment she saw something out of the ordinary. It is essential for parents to understand the importance of early interven-tion. But only a vigilant parent who pays attention to the warning signs is going to understand this and act on it.

As in the previous case, a parental intervention may not be enough. That's when a *clinical intervention* must take place. If the child needs to come in to a clinical setting for an intervention and evaluation, I always encourage both parents to attend, if possible. If it's a single-parent household, many times I will ask the estranged parent to come as well. Unfortunately, that isn't always possible and we must settle with one parent.

During the initial evaluation I ask the children exactly why they are here, find out what took place, and listen to what's going on with them and how they feel about themselves. I'll ask these children in front of their parent or parents to be honest if they're using drugs. I ask them to tell me what kind and how often. If the children answer that they aren't using drugs, I'll ask the question again to confirm the answer. Then I'll explain that part of the evaluation includes a urine test. This gives the children a chance to be honest and usually they relent and confess to their drug usage then and there.

In the beginning I try to gather as much information as possible. I want to know how the child has been acting. I want to know why the child was brought to see us. After asking these questions of the child I will ask them of the parents and I look for differences. I ask the parents how much contact they have with the child and I try to find out how much time the family as a whole spends together. I will also want to find out from the parents some of the information that child will usually try to withhold from us. I want to find out if the parents recall any trauma with the child in early childhood, problems with the birth, any alcoholism in the family, and any disabilities. I want to know if the parents have any knowledge of physical or sexual abuse. I want to find out if there's been bed wetting, fire setting, cruelty to animals or a lot of defiance from their child. If so, I want to find out what type. I want to find out generally from the parents what they feel is going on with their child.

Is the child isolating himself? Is the child up all night, or not going to school? I'll also ask the parents if they believe their child has low self-esteem and why. Why do they think the child is down on himself? If the child is egotistical, I'll ask them why they believe that and could it be for narcissistic reasons? More importantly I'll also ask the parents how they discipline their child. Do they set consequences and boundaries for their child? Does the child get any type of positive reinforcement along with the discipline?

Through all of these questions I am evaluating not only the child, but the parents, and sometimes to see if the parents have a substance abuse problem themselves. I'll come out and ask the parents if they drink much or use drugs, explicit questions of a confrontational nature to evaluate the situation.

Parents shouldn't be afraid of the evaluation or clinical intervention. Many times parents may fear that coming into a clinical situation is to call their parenting skills into question. Some parents even fear that this will lead to an accusation of abuse or neglect. An occasional spanking is not necessarily an indication of abuse, nor is a time-out automatically an indication of neglect. Our goal is not to separate a family or cause trauma, but to heal a family and help parents enhance their parenting skills. In fact, our motto is "Helping families stay together."

We do this through a holistic approach. Different from most clinics, we try to get the entire family involved in a child's therapy not because we want to call the parenting into question, but because we want to help the troubled child and usually we find it helps if we can at least meet and understand the entire family. We do not believe in a cookie-cutter approach, but that the best way to help a family is to tailor the counseling to the individual and to the individual family. That's why in the initial evaluation we try to get as much information about the mental, physical, and behavioral aspects of the child and family as possible. How is the child doing in school, how did he or she do before? What are the child's sleeping habits?

We tell the parents that we expect them to be involved in our program with their child and we try to teach the family, if need be, how to set healthy boundaries and consequences while at the same time supporting their child. To do this I may spend some time digging in the parents' background to find out how they were treated by their own parents. Most of us can end up parenting the way we were parented; after all, no one gives you a parenting manual the day you pick up your child from the hospital. You parent the way you were taught, through trial and error and some base instincts. But, for the most part, *we only know what we're taught and what we've learned from our parents and, peripherally, through other adult role models.*

At the end of the initial evaluation, with the parents present, I will ask them if there's anything else they want to ask or say. After we clear that up, I will then escort the parents to the waiting room, and then sit with the child and again ask him or her to be honest and tell me everything he feels is relevant about why he is visiting us.

Besides honesty, which is what I'm initially looking for, I'm also looking to see which one of the parents, in a two-parent household, is providing most of the nurturing, or if it is equally distributed between the two. I'm also looking for apathetic parenting, or excessive criticism or any of the other parenting problems we've already outlined.

In the course of this evaluation and intervention I will sometimes administer tests to determine the child's primary intake. By that we mean, is the child visually oriented or something else? Does he or she react to seeing things on paper, or react better to feelings or to something he hears? Is it better to give them a hug, show them that they got an "A" on a term paper, or tell them that you care and love them? This helps us in building a treatment program because it tells the therapist how best to discipline and praise the child.

We also administer different anxiety and depression tests, which we score while the child is present. This gives us a handle on where the child's anxiety is coming from, and we can use the test scores and answers as a road map into the dynamic that's causing his low self-esteem. These tests can also be used to see if the child is a candidate for medication; sometimes we've sent children to the appropriate doctors to see if they can prescribe nonaddicting antianxiety or anti-depressant medication.

It's best to take a common-sense approach to all of these avenues, however. Some children will come to us extremely defiant, and won't participate in any testing or questioning. Then we have to rely a lot on what the parents tell us.

Here's a case in point: Mark came in to be evaluated with his parents after being caught with alcohol on a couple of occasions. Mark was uncooperative and downplayed his alcohol usage. He also said he wasn't into drugs or anything else. In talking with his parents, we were informed that Mark had a real problem sleeping and, because he was up all night, he often couldn't get to school on time. Mark's parents also told us their son had wild mood swings. Sometimes he was filled with energy and seemingly euphoric. A few minutes later he would be depressed to the point of crying. Mark had also apparently been spewing a lot of anger directed at his younger sisters, and getting physical with them. The parents also reported that Mark, who was then seventeen, had taken to threatening his parents. His mother, who was fairly religious, explained that her son had threatened to destroy cherished religious relics if he didn't get what he wanted.

This, of course, upset the parents greatly. It was natural to be concerned about drug abuse, but Mark wouldn't say anything and remained aloof from all of us. We gave him a urine test which came back negative except for alcohol. Then we sent him out for a psychiatric evaluation. There it was discovered that his wild mood swings and other activities were symptomatic of a bipolar disorder. He was medicated, stabilized and has gone on to do very well, no longer abusing his siblings, parents, or alcohol.

The point, again, is to get as much information as you can in the initial intervention or evaluation. Any clinician who thinks he's seen it all and offers a quick diagnosis without going through all the facts is not a clinician worth seeing.

Another point worth making is that parents sometimes lose control, for whatever reason, of their children. Perhaps it is a single-parent family, or the father is always on the road, or the parents don't care. When they come to a clinical setting, one of the first things we try to do is reestablish some kind of hierarchy wherein the parents retain control. This we do by confronting the children and reminding them they are minors and their parents are legally responsible for them. It is amazing how thankful some parents are for this direct confrontation and how soon they will pick the ball back up and run with it. Sometimes the parents just need another adult to help them reestablish control.

In the initial evaluation I try to be very specific and leave nothing to chance. This not only helps in getting the proper information but also enables us to find which therapist is the best match for the child. Sometimes we want a therapist of the same gender as the subject, and sometimes it is better to get someone of the opposite gender. I am also very specific with my instructions in order to cut down on the chance of a misunderstanding and help the communication process between the parent and the child.

Ultimately, one of the things families have to understand about clinical interventions is that they must effect a change into the family dynamic. There is no way around it. If the family is healthy as a whole, then there is little chance they will be at our clinic in the first place. When we see families it is because of a problem with either the child or the parent.

So we go in and change the dynamic and try to help families become healthy. The problem is that change can be very uncomfortable for some people. Some people resent and resist change to the point that the entire family dynamic is in danger of collapsing. We deal with these cases with humor, discipline, love, acceptance, and perseverance. In that way the clinical intervention is not so different from the intervention of the parent. We usually only have to step in when the parents cannot or will not help themselves.

That is why we believe the whole family should be involved. But the bottom line is that no parent should ever fear to have a therapist involved.

CHAPTER 13
Nutritional factors

"I know a good diet can help my daughter,
but how can I get her to eat right?"

STRESS AND THE RIGORS THAT CAUSE LOW SELF-ESTEEM and depression take horrendous tolls on the body. Stress depletes a lot of nutrients your body needs to sustain itself and puts pressure on your body systems that can cause all kinds of physical harm. This, itself, can lead to a vicious cycle because the more stressed you are, the more you run your body down, and the more you become run down, the more stress you feel, and so the more you run your body down...ad infinitum.

The way children in the drug culture harm themselves is not only through the drugs they use, but in the way drugs act as a short-cut, stimulating the various brain centers and depleting valuable nutrients to it. Think of it as a turbo boost. You get the extra kick, but at the end you've depleted your reserves. That's exactly what children involved in abusing alcohol and drugs do to their bodies. That's also one of the reasons these children can be prone to colds and other maladies. They depress their immune system, run down their bodies, and thus leave themselves open to all kinds of infection.

In alcoholics, it seems that even years into recovery the damage the alcohol has done is plainly visible. Through our treatment and my work in the field I've noticed that heart disease and cancer seem to plague recovering alcoholics, even after the alcoholic has many years of sobriety under his belt. Clearly, the emotional toll of the drugs harms the physical condition of the addict or recovering addict. Many times a horrible diet is part of the reason. Alcoholics and drug addicts do not often care about what they put into their body for nutrition any more than they care what they put into their bodies for recreation.

Among the worst are those addicted to methamphetamines. The process of making and curing such drugs can involve the introduction of aluminum foil into a mixture that dissolves the foil. That mixture, once cured, is smoked or injected into the blood stream. "Speed freaks" are often emaciated, demonstrate poor physical hygiene, and probably haven't eaten for days. These addicts often look many years older than their age and demonstrate a complete lack of interest in physical maintenance. Obviously people who ingest or inject dissolved aluminum foil into their bodies care little about their physical maintenance.

Cocaine addicts have similar experiences. Cocaine also depletes the chemicals in your brain so well that it takes more and more of the drug over time to experience a high. It also drives the "crashes" cocaine addicts experience to even greater depths. I found this out first-hand after I entered recovery for a chemical dependence, and it is an experience that gives me a greater understanding of the addict's mind when we treat him or her in therapy.

I was in pretty sad shape after kicking my dependence on cocaine. I was basically unemployable. I had no concentration, and little ability to learn or remember anything. As part of my recovery I did a lot of research into diet and nutrition and what I found was that a lot of the old wives' tales hold true. If you want a good night's sleep, drink a glass of warm milk. The chemicals in the milk relax you and help you sleep. Fish, the old wives' tale says, is good brain food. As it turns out, it is. But, you don't have to look up old wives' tales. In therapy we recommend that parents get their children to a doctor for a physical exam and ask the doctor what nutrients and vitamins should be supplemented in a daily diet to help the child's immune system and also help get rid of all the toxic waste and byproducts that are in their child's system because of whatever chemical the child has been abusing.

Recent studies also indicate this is sound advice for those who are addicted to gambling and suffer from obsessive-compulsive disorders. Gamblers are under as much stress as alcoholics or cocaine addicts and that stress can compromise the body's immune system. The proper nutrition and diet can go a long way to help these people. It is important to get to a qualified doctor or nutritionist to set up the proper diet for your child and to maintain that diet. Several years of chemical abuse cannot be nullified overnight, but you will be amazed at how quickly a good diet, in combination with therapy and exercise, will help a child suffering from dependence or abuse.

The child who has become dependent on alcohol, gambling, drugs, or other people has been doing what we call "depleting the reservoir" of vitamins and amino acids necessary to maintain a healthy body. If you want to go for the gold in recovery, I often recommend a naturopathic physician or nutritionist to help a child get the right diet.

With all of this said, however, we can make some recommendations and offer a general guideline for vigilant parents to follow in maintaining their children and their health.

To begin with, there is nothing more important than setting a good example. If a parent is eating right, chances are the child will follow suit. Family Court in New Jersey's Middlesex County has a judge who preaches this very philosophy. Whenever a child is brought before the court the judge encourages the child and the parents to start each day with a good breakfast following a good night's sleep. He has mentioned numerous studies about how important it is to break the fast from sleeping with a good healthy meal. Without it, he talks of how hard it is to be alert in school or function well throughout the day.

In our clinic we believe and teach similar concepts. It is important for children to eat well and it is important for adults to set the standard by which they expect their children to live. It is hard to be a serious addict if you're getting eight hours of sleep and eating a healthy breakfast every morning. These two things are absolute cornerstones to good mental and physical health.

During the school year parents may seemed overwhelmed with getting their children ready for school, getting food on their plates, and having enough time to shower, shave, and get ready for work themselves. Still, if it takes an extra fifteen or thirty minutes in the morning I urge parents to make the sacrifice—to get up a bit earlier while going to bed a little sooner. Don't start the day off harried if at all possible. We live in a very fast-paced world, but slow it down enough to eat a good breakfast and to take time to greet and talk with family members in the morning. It isn't just the food that is important, but how you eat the food and how you begin your day.

This is part of our holistic approach to treating families. For the more time you take for the family up front before any trouble surfaces, the greater the chance that you will have fewer problems to confront. Use breakfast as a chance to not only put the right food in your body, but to put the right food in your child's mind. Talk with them about the coming day, what is going on in school, your children's interests. Anything. Connect and catch up and set an agenda for the day. Homework, tests, girl troubles, the big football game, anything and everything you feel comfortable talking about should be discussed at the morning breakfast table. Set boundaries if there are things you'd rather discuss later.

Lunch can be a problematic meal for the family since parents are at work and children are at school. So I thoroughly recommend a family gathering around the dinner table. As you use the breakfast table to set up an agenda for the day, so use the dinner table to reconnect with your family. Find out how things went at school, check back in, give them updates on your life. Stay connected. Stay focused on the family. This doesn't have to be as rigid as Barbara Billingsley dressed in pearls serving her family a steaming pot roast on *Leave It to Beaver* while she admonishes her husband Ward for "being a little rough on the Beaver," but it should have a natural feel to it. Adapt these strategies to your own family and apply them as you see fit in order to gain the most from them. A good diet can have a therapeutic effect on the child and the family as a whole, and a full meal eaten at leisure while the family spends time together is a great aid to the family. Strive to eat at least one meal a day, if not two, as a family unit. You can expect some resistance to this idea from adolescents who believe you're either cramping their style or butting in where you don't belong.

To those children I say, "Tough." On one level the children may resist this disciplined approach to getting the family together, but on another they'll appreciate the concern and attention you're giving them. Think of the other dividends this pays in your relationship with your children. How well can a child hide a gambling, alcohol, drug, or co-dependence problem if she is under the scrutiny of her parents the first thing in the morning for breakfast and later during dinner? Also, by getting together for meals, the parents are reaffirming the hierarchal nature of the family. The parents are in control and the children are expected to participate in the family hierarchy. The parents are, in a subtle manner, showing their children who is the boss simply by being present. This keeps the children further down the line from bucking that authority; they see it maintained on a daily basis.

Spending time to eat with your children may also cut down on the need to snack in between meals. Some children actually use food as a way to deal with their low self-esteem. Of course, the more they eat, the larger they become and the more depressed they get and thus the more they eat. Parents who are in control of their child's diet can, to some extent, avoid this type of self-destructive behavior.

Parents also should shop wisely for food. My father, who was also my first football coach, used to react loudly to the use of "belly wash," which is what he called the empty calories of soda, candy bars, Twinkies, Ho-Ho's, Ding-Dongs, and a variety of other sweet treats that children love. By refusing to buy this type of food most parents can effectively and significantly cut down the chances that their children will indulge themselves in unhealthy food habits.

Thinking of nutrition and how important it is to maintain your health brings me to the story of Joe. I met Joe about fourteen years ago when he needed to detox from heroin. Joe told me during the course of our first interview that he had been shooting heroin steadily for twenty years. During this time he had gotten hepatitis C and the HIV virus.

Joe didn't do well after his first detox effort and relapsed. He came back for a second, third, and fourth attempt. The results were always the same; he fell back into his old, familiar ways. Then, suddenly after his fifth attempt at sobering up, Joe got it right. The difference, he claimed, was not only treatment, but NA meetings, exercise, and nutrition.

He researched and set up his own regimen for maintaining his health which included a good amount of juice. In fact, he was so infatuated with his juice therapy that he spoke about it at Narcotics Anonymous meetings and to anyone else that would listen. He became known as "Joe Juice" to certain people, and to this day he has maintained his sobriety, years after his last detox.

It wasn't just the nutrition, although that certainly is a big part of it. It was the good habits he formed from his research. It was his maintaining a daily regimen of eating the proper foods and the work he had to undertake to get the proper nutrition. It became a ritual, almost a religion, which is to say, in the terms of many twelve-step programs, he turned his life over to a higher authority. To do this Joe ingested carrots, celery, apples, garlic, parsley, spinach, and assorted vitamins with the same vigor he once reserved for his drug addiction. Perhaps some would argue that he merely substituted one addiction for another. But he also began exercising by taking long walks, and that, combined with the nutrition, allowed him to turn his life around. During the past fourteen years Joe has seen many of his contemporaries in NA succumb to drugs, but Joe just keeps on juicing, taking supplements, walking, and living his life.

Joe's experience also calls upon the need for another type of nutrition. We've skirted around the edges of it in speaking of family rituals and Joe's need to turn his life over to a higher authority, but the simple fact is that the body also needs spiritual nutrition. Often addicts have neglected this part of their diet as well.

At the core of many twelve-step programs is the third step, which says that the addict will make a decision to turn his will and his life over to the care of God as he "understands him." This nondenominational yet very spiritual portion of the program is essential nutrition for the upkeep of the body. Recent articles in various magazines have outlined how our brain seems to be wired to accept God or the concept of a deity. One may argue about who wired our brain in such a manner, but it is no longer relevant to argue why we need spiritual nourishment. The fact is, we need it.

It is important that parents understand this. You cannot ignore the need for spiritual nourishment any more than you can ignore the need for a good amount of fiber in your diet. Just as we do not try to sell parents on any particular brand of fiber for their child, we also are not missionaries for any particular brand of faith. Each parent must decide how and what to teach his or her children about God, but it cannot be ignored.

Again, by spending the time to do this, parents are reaffirming the family hierarchy. Also, parents who are interested in teaching their children about God usually don't take a "whatever" approach to their child's life. Parents who teach their child about God also give the child an ability to reach out to God for whatever reason the child may need later on in life. Perhaps the respect, fear or mere presence of God in the life of children will be enough to keep them from becoming addicts. Perhaps it is the presence of God in their life that will help children maintain a high self-esteem level through familiar childhood traumas. Whatever the case, it is a tool that has been neglected by many parents today. For many reasons it has become fashionable to take God out of everything. Yet, the mere concept of God helps establish moral guidelines and enhances conscience and character.

I have seen many instances in which prayer and the belief in God have helped someone overcome the worst drug-addicted conditions. It matters not whether you worship in a mosque, a church, a synagogue, or at the feet of Buddha. What does matter is a thorough grounding in some belief system. It is up to each individual to discover the concept of God, and to grow spiritually. However, it is up to parents to feed their children spiritually as they do physically.

Some people may consider this preaching, but religion in general and the very concept of God have lost a lot of ground in our culture. Certainly it is not a priority, and many parents may choose to ignore this part of their child's nutritional needs because they may have experienced or read about instances of the hypocrisy in religious people.

But as the saying goes, "Don't throw the baby out with the bath water." Our therapy is based on the concept that every child is born into this world with a birthright to be loved, respected, and valued. In turn, every child born into this world must exhibit the same. We seem to have forgotten this precept as we begin the third millennium. We were taught as children that "God didn't make junk," but today people often treat each other as if they were just that.

In movie theaters when I was growing up, along with the usual previews, the theaters used to put up a sign on the screen that said, "The family that worships together stays together." Television stations used to broadcast each night the public service announcement, "It's eleven o'clock. Parents, do you know where your children are?"

These little nods to the need of spiritual nourishment aren't often seen today and that is not a legacy we should be proud to pass on to our children. If you feed your children the proper nutrition they will grow up to be very healthy adults indeed.

The bottom line is that it is the parents' responsibility to serve their children not only the proper physical nourishment, but spiritual nourishment as well.

CHAPTER 14
Benefits of exercise

"All my child does all day is sit in front of the television. I can't get him to move."

REALLY? WELL, THE TELEVISION IS A WONDERFUL INVENTION that doesn't need a v-chip, and doesn't need to be programmed to keep your children from accessing porno and HBO. It has all the censoring, monitoring, and parental controls it needs in one simple button: the on/off switch. Use it.

Actually, the complaint by parents is a common one, but it isn't just about television any more. Any number of parents complain daily about how their children are seemingly addicted to video games, play stations, and numerous hand-held computer devices that may improve hand-to-eye coordination but do very little else. It is therefore important to make sure that children are involved in some daily physical exercise regimen to help keep them in good physical and emotional shape.

Exercise can be essential to the recovering addict, and those adults most successful at recovery usually have worked out some sort of exercise regimen. Exercise helps a child look better and get into better shape, and thereby begins to bolster the child's self-esteem. It helps build stamina and boosts energy levels so the child will feel better. It gives the body a natural high, which can help keep the child from getting involved in other, more deleterious activities.

Exercise itself can be a great way to keep children from self-destructing by the use of drugs or becoming addicted to gambling. It's contradictory to be involved in self-care and exercise and at the same time use drugs and become self-destructive. (Darryl Strawberry and other professional athletes with drug problems may be exceptions that prove the rule, but adults are not children and their problems with drugs can be vastly different from those of a child.)

Getting a child involved in exercise early and regularly is invaluable. The secret to building self-esteem is focusing on confidence and self-respect. Good exercise boosts confidence and endurance. You strengthen yourself physically, which in turn can strengthen you mentally.

Think of the exercise regimen. Taking merely fifteen minutes a day and focusing on cardiovascular exercise, be it running or calisthenics, is fifteen minutes when you are forced to focus on activities that enhance your well-being. You're not going to be smoking crack or drinking alcohol, gambling or worried about your lover or anything else except the exercise for that specific time. There is an almost Zen-like clarity that comes with focusing on nothing but counting your jumping jacks or push-ups or putting one foot in front of the other as you strive to finish a mile run. Not only do you build up a sweat, but your body flushes out toxins and so does your mind as you struggle along physically.

It is important for children to be involved in organized sports also. In so doing, children become involved with other children who are sober, aren't worried about or doing drugs, and are focused on a common goal. My wife and I have three sons and we encourage them to be involved in sports year-round. You can, of course, take this too far, and I've seen parents spend all their time shuttling their children back and forth between soccer, football, and baseball games all in one season. I encourage parents to limit the child to one sport per season.

Parents should be encouraged to follow other recommendations for sports. Allow your son or daughter to be coached by his or her coach. Do not interfere. Be a good parent and encourage your child and others in a positive manner. Treat each player, opposing coach, official, parent, and others in the area with respect and dignity. Do your best to learn the fundamental rules and strategies of the sport. This is important; I've often seen parents, misguided in their criticism, do more harm than good by screaming out and calling "foul" when none has taken place. Youth soccer is especially conducive to this behavior. Most parents never played the sport themselves and consequently have little idea what is going on. One of my favorite stories as a coach is when a parent approached me after practice one day. "You don't like my son very much," she said. I was shocked, for the boy was one of the best forwards on the soccer team and had scored most of our goals. "Why do you say that?" I asked. She said, "Well, I noticed you never let my son pick up the ball, but you always let that other boy pick up the ball," she said pointing to my goalie. I had to inform her politely that the goalie was the only child allowed to pick up the ball on the field. She just looked at me in disbelief.

Organized sports, in addition to being a great way for a child to get a healthy dose of exercise on a regular basis, is also a place for parents to socialize. Take the opportunity to get to know the other parents on the team. Be great spectators and do everything possible to make the experience fun for everybody. Support the authority of officials who are assigned to the contests and assist them in every way to conduct fair and impartial competitive contests. Help protect the health and safety of the players by insisting that all activities be conducted for the players' psychological and physiological welfare. This is important because some youth sports programs emphasize a "win at any cost" attitude. We all like to win, but I urge parents to shop around to find the best program for their child. Some are more competitive and more talented than others. You will do your child a great favor by finding a program suited to his or her desires, goals, and abilities.

At the beginning of every football season I tell the parents in our program that most of the children who play youth tackle football will never play high school, college, or professional football. This will be their only experience playing organized football. So we strive to make it an enjoyable experience for all the children and urge parents to do the same. This is very important because the competitive nature of organized sports can enhance, but can also hurt, self-esteem. Programs in which children are berated, belittled, yelled at, or otherwise treated inappropriately can lead to a destruction of self-esteem and therefore cause more harm than good.

Look for coaches who set an example. Parents should set one themselves. Many times over the years I've seen parents use organized sports as a substitute baby sitter. By that I mean that parents will drop their child off at practice or even games and never stay to be involved in their child's activity. The greatest joy as a coach is watching a child excel and then seeing the look of joy on his face as he does so. The child at that moment misses something if his parents are not around.

An excellent example of this is a young child we'll call Lawrence. Lawrence came out for football and was small and athletic, but didn't have any experience playing the sport. At the beginning of the year he wasn't doing very well and his parents stopped coming to see him practice and play. Lawrence became dejected, but we hung with him and encouraged him as coaches. Then one day Lawrence got into a game, scooped up a fumble in the end zone, and scored a touchdown. He was ecstatic. But his ecstasy quickly turned to sadness when he realized his father and mother weren't there to watch his moment of triumph. He quit the team shortly thereafter—because, he said, no one cared whether or not he played. The coaches did, but he needed his parents.

Parents can make up all kind of excuses for not getting involved in their child's life, some legitimate and some not. But each year when parents tell me they can't spend any time helping our football team, I ask them what is going on in their life that is more important than their own children. I emphasize that they can make an outing out of each fall football Saturday. Get all of the kids together, watch the game, and do something as a family. Sometimes that argument works and sometimes it falls on deaf ears.

It is a struggle; with three children of my own, I know this, but I've seen over the years that the children who are the most confident and do best in school and in life have the solid support of their family behind them.

Exercise and organized sports can be a cornerstone to the healthy self-esteem children need.

In organized sports, we hope children will be hanging around with the right kind of people while filling their time away from drugs and alcohol. It becomes something to look forward to as the child struggles to improve his performance. These children are not left with a lot of idle time on their hands. They don't become bored easily and they have energy to get things done. They sleep better, they take care of themselves better, and consequently they feel better about themselves.

In every sport I've ever coached, I've also stressed the idea of team play and cooperation. Children get a sense of becoming part of something bigger than themselves and they get the feeling they can work and get along with others. They are accepted by a peer group with a positive outlook and goal. Rather than seeking the acceptance of peers who are into drugs and questionable behavior they are spending time with children who are in a sober environment engaged in healthy activities. The most important thing for someone who is suffering from low self-esteem or for a child who's involved in substance abuse is to be active in a sober, healthy living situation and not have a lot of idle time on his or her hands.

The drug culture has its own ritual of copping, or buying, drugs, hanging out with dealers and friends, partying, and getting high. By substituting that unhealthy ritual with a healthy one of organized sports or exercise, parents will do their child a lot of good.

Some believe that sports is for "dumb jocks" or "squares," and that organized sports or exercise is detrimental to a child's well-being. But how many children will brag about their drug use or be feted by their peers for using the most marijuana or heroin in a day? Not many. Yet we do fete the athlete in every sport I've been involved with, and we teach the children that they cannot play unless they do well in school. It goes hand in hand.

The term "organized sports" can be a fairly loose term that describes many different exercise activities. It can be Tae-Kwan-Do, football, or fencing...or just about anything else. Take the case of James. He was sixteen years old. He was drinking a lot and using marijuana almost daily. His self-esteem was about nil as he tried to come to grips with his drug and alcohol problems. He wanted to be more than he was, but didn't know how to go about it.

His problem was his weight. Like many children we see these days, James had a weight problem, which fueled his low self-esteem. His problem, fueled by a poor diet and a complete lack of physical activity, only became worse the more alcohol and marijuana he ingested.

James and his parents sought our help, and once we got him into therapy and he stopped taking drugs and alcohol, his weight began to stabilize. But the weight really began to come off when James got involved at a local gym. The camaraderie, the organized efforts he undertook, all helped him to get into much better physical condition. Even though James wasn't involved in an organized sport like basketball, he was involved in a daily ritual that involved sports and exercise, and that helped him build his confidence and self-respect.

Eventually James lost about sixty pounds. He went on to a career in physiology and became a personal trainer. It was the organized exercise and sporting environment that helped him to become who he wanted to be.

Many times we find that children don't feel comfortable about their looks and their weight and that in itself can lead to problems of low self-esteem. They can come from what many would consider "normal" families, but at the same time there's something not normal with these obese children. The problem, of course, goes back to the apathetic parent in most cases. By using television, the Internet, computer games, and Nintendo as baby sitters, we've given rise to a whole generation of increasingly obese and moribund children who have little or no physical ability and consequently little or no self-esteem.

There has even been a hue and a cry against physical activity and in particular organized sports from some parents who complain of the competitive nature of sports and the bad behavior that accompanies such organized activities. While it is true and deplorable that some youth organized sporting activities lead to arguments and even physical altercations (usually among the parents, not the children), it is ridiculous to dismiss what is good about the competitive nature of sports because of what is bad. Better sportsmanship can be taught to parents and children. What all of them must realize is that the organized sporting activity is *for the children.* It is not for the parents to relive their childhood nor to live vicariously through their children. If that could be remembered then 99 percent of the problems of youth sporting events would evaporate.

Still, organized sports may not be the appropriate exercise for some children. A simple exercise regimen may be the best way to help them out. A daily regimen of fifteen minutes of exercise, including sit-ups, jumping jacks, push-ups, leg stretches, etc., may be an excellent way to focus the mind and the body. The repetition of such exercise alone can help a child's confidence level immensely. When I coach young people today, I recommend such a regimen. Here's what I recommend children do at home, twice a day:

1. 20 jumping jacks
2. 10 push-ups
3. 30 sit-ups
4. 1 minute of "hurdler" stretches
5. 1 minute of "butterfly" stretches

6. 2 minutes of running in place

7. 20 jumping jacks

The idea behind the workout is just to get the kids up and doing something. These are not strenuous exercises, but I have found they will get the child thinking about exercise and their physical and mental hygiene.

Other methods can be just as successful. Another young client was Billy. He suffered from low self-esteem that was fueled by being picked on in school early in his life. He was often put down and called a nerd. It was difficult for Billy to handle the cutting remarks of his peers and he felt uncomfortable with who he was. So Billy retreated into a fantasy world fueled by his increasing infatuation with marijuana and other drugs.

We worked with Billy in therapy for a while and then suggested that he get involved in some sort of exercise regimen to help out his self-esteem and to give him a chance to stand up for himself. He decided to take karate. After getting involved in this he began to work out vigorously.

I cannot tell you how much the discipline of karate or Tae-Kwan-Do can help a young child. These martial arts are disciplined regimens by their very nature and they demand that the students show proper respect to authority and work hard to be honest in everything they do.

This particular regimen was extremely effective for Billy. He began to feel good about himself; he gained confidence and self-respect. Soon he didn't entertain thoughts of being powerless, nor did he find himself needing to retreat into fantasies or drugs to find a place where he could be happy. He entered and won competitions, and the gratifying highs he got from physical exertion, coupled with the increase in self-esteem, helped him to kick his old debilitating habits. He ate better, he lived better, he felt better, and ultimately Billy did a lot of good for himself.

As we can see, diet and exercise really go hand in hand. In organized sports we stress that children who want to excel need to eat right, and those who eat right want to exercise to get the most benefit out of the proper diet.

The most important thing for people to understand is that you cannot motivate people into action. If people wait for the proper motivation to get into action, i.e., proper diet and exercise, it isn't going to happen, especially if they are suffering from low self-esteem or drug abuse. Those stimuli cause lethargic behavior and there isn't a lot of motivation to do the right thing for your body. What we try to do is get people to understand that action creates motivation. Do not wait to get motivated because it might not happen for awhile—especially if you're suffering from low self-esteem and you're trying to kick a gambling, drug, or other addictive habit.

Instead, get into action and that action will create its own motivation. For example, you may not want to wash your car, but you know once you start washing it, you automatically become motivated to finish it. You may not want to clean your desk or file your papers, and you may not be motivated to do it, but once you start to do it, again, you become motivated to finish the task.

Who wants to get up and start the proper exercise regimen? But once we get out on the track, or get to the gym, or join an organized sport, we find that we eventually feel good about ourselves. This, in turn, provides the motivation to continue the behavior. This is where parents can come in—by encouraging and empowering the child to get involved and continue an exercise program until the child's own motivation kicks in.

A final note on the subject of exercise: inasmuch as one cannot ignore the need for spiritual nourishment, one also cannot ignore the need for spiritual exercise. This may come in many different forms, and it isn't necessarily restricted to a visit to a church or a synagogue or a mosque. There are many ways to exercise one's spiritual needs, whether it is reading the Bible or the Koran, doing volunteer work, or even cleaning up and assisting workers at your local place of worship.

Each year, for example, I get my children to spend at least one day working in a soup kitchen or putting together their old toys and clothes and taking them to a mission where they volunteer time. My idea is simply to get them to exercise their faith a bit. I also believe that it gives the disenfranchised child living in suburbia a harsh dose of reality. Many times I've seen that children involved in drugs and suffering from low self-esteem really have no idea of the breaks they have, of how fortunate they are. I believe exercising their faith strengthens children's self-esteem and makes them a little more thankful for what they do have.

CHAPTER 15
Building self-worth

"As hard as I try, I just cannot get my child to believe in himself. What can I do?"

IT STARTS AT HOME AND IT STARTS WITH THE PARENTS. After we're born, but even before conscious memory, we put our parents on a pedestal. So parents have a large effect on their child's self-esteem. One of the most important ways children can feel good about themselves is when they feel they are valuable to their parents. At a very young age, children are unsure of themselves and their parents can help bolster their fragile ego by showing faith in them, even when giving good, but never mean-spirited, criticism.

I use organized sports again as an example. On the football field I've noticed two types of coaches. They both may be emotional, they both may raise their voices, but one does it to be heard and the other does it to pick. The best coach I ever saw was a coach who took a kid aside who'd just been "beat" on a sweep. "It's okay, everybody makes mistakes," he told the kid. "I still believe in you. Go get 'em." The other coach screamed, yelled, and took a kid out who'd made a similar mistake. "You let your whole team down," that coach yelled. "You have no business out on the field."

Now, I ask you, which child is going to try harder next time, and which child is going to feel good about himself? Now, perhaps you realize how important a child's parents are in the process of child development.

The next step in building self-worth, after spending time with the child is allowing the child to communicate in a honest and open manner. Do not demean them, even if what the child says seems ignorant or perhaps even stupid to you the parent. Facts may have little to do with feelings, so you can allow the child to communicate their feelings, you can even validate those feelings and understand them, but you do not have to believe the facts the child presents to you are valid. Indeed, you as a parent may want to point out to the child in the context of an open discussion why you believe their feelings may be based on misinformation in order to help them gain a foothold on reality and a greater self-esteem.

My favorite example of this comes from my own son. He grew up with a friend, and was very close with the boy. Then by the third grade we moved away. We moved back to the same neighborhood two years later and the two boys found they were not that close any more. "He doesn't like me," my son explained. "He's always making fun of me." My wife and I happened to be good friends with the boy's parents, and I found that his former friend was expressing the exact same sentiment to his parents. Both boys' feelings were valid for them, but based on erroneous facts. The boys had different interests and while they became good friends again, it wasn't the same as when they had been preschoolers. They couldn't understand this difference at their age and had we allowed it to progress, it could have caused problems for both boys. But allowing my son a forum to express his feelings without his parents saying something like, "You're nuts" or "What's wrong with you?" gave him confidence to not only be open with us about other issues, but made him understand there was nothing wrong with the feelings he had, but that he should try to get all of the facts before he jumped to a conclusion.

The best way to listen is in an atmosphere of unconditional love. "Because I love you, it's okay. I understand how you feel, but I want you to understand all of the facts, or Mom and Dad's point."

In a clinical setting we often advise parents on the correct way to institute, among other things, a working curfew. "Because I love you I understand what you're saying and how you're feeling; however, I want you to understand why your mother and father want you in earlier. We just can't give in here. These are the rules and regulations."

We urge parents to use this method of communication. You have to be firm about the rules, but allow the child time to express his feelings. The child feels part of the process, less slighted and more likely to go along with the program. We don't counsel parents to give in nor to be the type of parent who easily gives in under the guise of allowing the child "his space." Old-fashioned discipline works, but a sense of communication with the child helps. The old adage "a spoonful of sugar" does often help the strict medicine of discipline to go down much more smoothly and allows the child a chance to build his or her self-esteem. If children think they are valued and can talk with their parents, then many a larger problem can be avoided or cured in its infancy.

You must tell your child that "I love you no matter what. I may disagree with you. I may set boundaries, I may oppose what you do or say. I may punish you or set consequences, but I do these things because I love you. Not to be mean. Not be hurtful, or exercise demeaning control over you. Also because I love you, I want to teach you. I want to encourage you. I want to point you in the right direction. I want to help you deal with life and support you and help you get through adolescence. I want to teach you to balance your life. You don't have to be perfect, but I expect you to give your best shot and try your best.

"Because I love you, I will let you face life and its consequences. You will be allowed to try things on trial and error. You can turn failure and pain into learning experiences."

All of these things help the child help themselves. Confidence is earned, as is self-esteem. It is earned by what the child puts into his or her activities and what they get back from them. Mom and Dad can help out, but it is important for a child to learn they can't score a touchdown every time and they may not always win, but they always try their hardest and they learn from their mistakes. That's what builds confidence.

If someone does everything for you and you're unable to try yourself and fail, how can you have good confidence and good self-esteem? If somebody does everything for you and spoils you and won't allow you to assume responsibility for your actions, how can you not only build confidence or self-esteem but learn the very basics needed to survive as an adult in society? You must learn there are consequences for your actions, and that good decisions beget good results. The only time you fail is when you stop trying.

So to the woman who writes that she's tried everything to help her child build self-esteem and nothing seems to work, we say, keep trying. Don't quit. One thing may not work. Another attempt may not work, but the effort is the result. You will get better if you continue trying, and the simple act of trying continues to build confidence.

I think it is also important for parents to keep a mind toward positive reinforcement for a job well done. We're looking for progress, not perfection.

Procrastination must be avoided in this effort. It is the deadliest of sins as far as building good self-esteem. The children get the message that someone will solve their problems for them, so why should the child try at all? If the child has a history of procrastination and it's become cemented in their psyche via learned behavior from the parents, it's going to be very hard for the child later in life because they've never been independent. They won't be confident and they'll always look for someone to bail them out of whatever negative situation in which they find themselves. So, it's very important for parents to keep an eye on procrastination.

As children get older, the more they procrastinate, the more things will build up. The more things that don't get done, the more the child will feel stress, guilt, and low self-esteem and they'll begin to feel like a failure.

To combat procrastination the parent must set up boundaries and consequences. Policing your child may not be the most thrilling job you'll do as a parent, but it will bring you great benefits as your child gets older. Make sure your child does his homework. Make sure they clean up their room. Make sure they wash daily, learn to do their laundry as they get older and implement curfews that are not arbitrary. Give the child a sense that they have expectations and limitations. These guidelines will not only help battle procrastination, but much of what a parent can and should be willing to do can battle all sorts of other problems and help a child, ultimately, to feel better about themselves.

For parents it may not always be readily apparent that what they are doing in any way leads to a child feeling better about themselves. Often it may seem that in setting rigid guidelines children and the parents see nothing but pain and torture in the process. For the parent it may be easier to let the five-year-old stay up later. They fuss less, they are easier to get along with and what, really, does it matter if the child isn't in school? Children who get their way are easier to handle, and ultimately they will probably fall asleep before the parent.

But, the danger is that children can get the idea from the lax parenting that not only do they get to do what they want, but mom and dad don't think much of them because they let them do whatever they want. This feeling, not often expressed, will then be tested by the child in other parts of their life and through other, and usually increasingly inappropriate, behavior. The child who thinks their parents do not hold them in value, particularly younger children, will have a harder time than others in building their self-worth.

It is far better for children to face consequences, especially for procrastination, earlier in life rather than later. The earlier a parent intervenes, as we've said before, the earlier the recalcitrant behavior will be dealt with and ultimately the easier and quicker the problem will be solved.

The parent has to make sure the child is emotionally healthy, and must help early on in getting the child to have a healthy self-esteem.

This takes persistence. Persistence pays off. Give me a persistent person over a supposedly extremely intelligent person any time, any day, anywhere. The persistent person will eventually succeed, but the procrastinator, even if extremely intelligent, will not. There are no failures with persistence, only learning experiences. Or, as John Lennon said, there are no problems, only solutions. In this regard, and at the risk of using another cliché, persistence can be its own reward. Children who persist will accomplish great things and it is very important that a child persist even without success. This is why it becomes its own reward. If the child waits for a high self-esteem or some motivation in order to persist, then he may never do so. The child who merely jumps in and persists will do so, eventually, out of habit. The self-esteem therefore comes from the persistence, not the other way around. It is important as parents to get your child into the habit of persisting, against any odds, early.

The most effective assistance a parent can provide in this regard is to support and monitor the child's behavior. While no parent wants to encourage their child to beat their head up against a wall—after all, that is a form of persistence—the parent wants to encourage the child to evaluate and persist where prudent. If the child loves to play football, for example, then the parent would be wise to encourage the child to continue to play even if the child is having a difficult time playing the game, as long as the child is enjoying himself. It isn't logical nor prudent for a parent to force the child to play against their will, nor is it wise for a parent to urge the child to persistently pursue the sport if the child has no initial interest in it. I've seen parents destroy their child's self-worth by forcing them into situations the child has no aptitude for nor desire to participate in, simply because the parent wants the child to be there—in some cases because the parent wants to live vicariously through the child.

The parent is not doing anyone any good by forcing a child into a situation the child has no desire to be in simply because the parent wishes it to be. Parental discretion is not only advised but mandatory in this regard. In order to help our children we, as parents, must constantly evaluate our own behavior and ask ourselves if what we are asking of our children, or demanding of them, is simply for ourselves and not the benefit of the child. This does not rule out stern discipline, nor love, but asks us to constantly ask if what we are doing will in some way not only do no harm, but actually provide a benefit to our child. It is a hard row to hoe, but children will recognize a parent who is making mistakes while trying to do well, as opposed to an apathetic parent who makes mistakes out of disregard for the child or for other more selfish or sinister motives.

A child without structure and support will fail as surely as a building will fall without a foundation. It is important, therefore, early on for parents to get ingrained the learned behavior that will best help the child survive. Once ingrained in the child they have a better chance of keeping this with them. This helps them to assert themselves and get ahead in life.

Educating your children thus becomes key. This starts by literally pulling out a dictionary and making a child understand the meaning of words like persistence, patience, assertiveness, discipline, and respect. To educate your child you must be able to communicate with them. To communicate thoroughly with a child be prepared to break things down to the child not only in terms they can understand, but in ways useful to them. My own educational experience with my youngest son illustrates this point.

He, his older brothers, and a few of their friends had built, staffed, managed, and operated their own lemonade stand one afternoon. The older children were constantly raiding the lukewarm drink, which was the primary merchandise at the stand. At one point my youngest son got extremely upset with the oldest and accused him of making off with all the merchandise he was struggling hard to sell. He was yelling and screaming and generally acting his age when I approached him. "Hey, you want to sell this stuff, right?" I asked neither yelling nor upset. He stopped. "Yes, Dad, I do, but he keeps drinking it all." The five-year-old exclaimed.

"Well, don't worry. You'll make plenty of money."

"How?"

"Well, we have a lot more lemonade in the house and your brother can't possibly drink all of it. So, you have an unlimited supply of lemonade. As long as someone makes it."

My youngest son indicated that was a fine idea as long as his older brother made the lemonade. Time passed. My middle son returned with a friend from an advanced lemonade stand sales trip at the semi-busy neighborhood intersection about 75 feet down the street. My middle son arrived to see my youngest son raiding the hitherto sacrosanct supply of lemonade. Now it was the middle son's turn to admonish the youngest about raiding the reverential lemonade supply. My youngest son was very cool and turned to the middle son and said, "What are you mad about, huh? We can always make more."

My middle son blinked and then smiled. "Cool. Let me have some."

My experience is not unique in parentdom. During the course of any normal day parents involved in their child's life will make dozens of decisions and communicate to their child in the exact appropriate manner many times without even thinking about it. I've seen this time and again in coaching, at school, at the swimming pool, shopping—in almost every situation imaginable. But it is ironic that, afterward, some parents don't even realize what they did, although their child does. It is harnessing these fleeting moments of good parenting and making a conscious effort to make those kinds of parenting decisions that is essential for all of us parents today.

Besides education, encouragement is invaluable in establishing faith in your children. Empty encouragement can be really harmful, but well-placed encouragement is very important in helping children establish a high self-esteem. At our agency we use a lot of it to make sure the children know the encouragement is because they are doing things right. We urge parents not to be perfectionists.

For example, if the child comes home with a B+ instead of an A on the report card, we tell parents not to be hypercritical. It's not perfection, but it took an effort to get the high grade. It helps a child to feel appreciated even if the child falls short—as long as the child is trying. This should not be pity, but encouragement. It goes a long way.

This brings to mind a client by the name of Ray. Ray came for counseling when he was sixteen years old. He was very big for his age and very good in basketball. He had been encouraged to play basketball since he was very young and in grade school. His dad was convinced it was his ticket to stardom and, in fact, as a high school sophomore he was on the first-string basketball team. He was the second leading scorer on the team and very much the hero of the team his father had always wanted. But the father was also a perfectionist. Practice, practice, practice made perfect. But nothing was ever good enough for the father.

That's not to say that the father didn't praise his son. He did. However, he used the word "but" each time. For example, he would say, "You were great in that game son, but you missed too many free throws." Or, "You had the most points, but you didn't guard your man." The word "but" negated every bit of praise the father had given the son. Parents have to be aware of this. To a child's ear they hear nothing but the criticism following the word "but." This sets the child up to feel that no matter how well he performs, there is nothing he can do right. In Ray's case he felt anxiety and low self-esteem and thus began to drink alcohol heavily. He missed practice, he faltered, and the father came to us for help.

We then worked with the father to ease up on the perfectionist behavior. The move couldn't have come at a better time because Ray's grades had dropped off significantly. He had been taking college preparatory courses and was extremely intelligent, but he was still only a kid and could only deal with so much pressure. We found that his alcohol and eventually substance abuse came from his feelings of stress brought on by his dad. By persuading the father to change his tactics, we helped Ray relieve his stress and thus he no longer felt the need to use and abuse substances.

In other ways parents can encourage a child. Let the children know it's okay to make a mistake and encourage them to do better. Let them know that learning to be adults will mean a certain amount of failure as they grow. Experiencing failure should not encourage a child to quit the struggle.

Since this chapter concerns building self-worth, we cannot slight the role the self plays in the process. We've spent time telling parents how they can help their children to increase their self-esteem, but we also need to address what children can do for themselves—even if their parents aren't there for them.

Children need to know they are not trash, disposable, unwanted, neglected, or abused. It seems like a given, but there are plenty of children who are treated this way. So parents, guardians, and even friends can assist and give guidance to children even if peripherally. Encouragement, recognition, and the continued support of accomplishments is something all adults can give. Think of it as giving back.

Some of the various self-help techniques that a child can do for himself include a positive affirmation where child stands in front of a mirror and says to himself that he deserves love and respect. Try it. Have a child stand in front of the mirror, look at himself and say, "I am a good person and I deserve love and respect."

This technique, satirized by Al Franken on *Saturday Night Live* many years ago, seems silly to some and repulsive to others. But the fact is that when done repeatedly the child begins to believe in himself. This experience should be augmented by the child saying it out loud, hearing the words. The child is already looking at himself and he should also hug himself. To a child of five or six this helps immensely. All of the senses are stimulated as the child engages in this practice. Sight, sound, and touch are all brought into play and this helps the child to remember and to act on these feelings. We recommend a child engage in this type of behavior eleven times a day for several weeks. Watch what happens. If this is done in combination with our recommendations, soon the child will program himself into believing in his own self-worth. He will then begin to take steps to enhance his self-esteem.

If they want to do it, do it and have some faith in it, it will be instilled in them. Self-respect is taught through this behavior, one of the cornerstones to good self-esteem. Another is confidence. A positive affirmation that will instill confidence is saying, "I am a good person and I will succeed at _____" and the blank should be filled in with whatever they want to do. If this is done in front of the mirror, too, it can help a child enormously to gain self-confidence.

A self-help written exercise helps children to know exactly what they want, how they're going to obtain it, and when. If they write this out, it will, again, help children to visualize and make possible the things they want.

As simple as these exercises look and sound, they can have a very profound effect on the child. We designed a little exercise for children for use in our practice. The idea is for the child to come to grips with preconceived notions, misinformation, and self-esteem issues. We call the exercise "Truth or Dare."

It's a variation of the old game, and based on other clinical exercises. We have the child take a piece of paper at the top of which is a blank box. We instruct the children to write a negative truth about themselves inside the box. Typically this statement is something like, "I am ugly," "I'm a loser," "I can't do anything right," "I'm going to end up in jail," and so on.

Underneath the box are the following headings which we "Dare" the children to apply to their written statement as a description of the statement. Those headings are:

COOL OR FOOL PERSON:

I have to be perfect in all I do, or I'm not cool. Guess what. Perfect doesn't exist. The greatest baseball player didn't get a hit every time at bat. Not all beautiful girls win a pageant or become models. No one has a perfect day every day of his life. Everyone has days when they don't look or feel well. And no one can please everybody all of the time.

LOSER PERSON:

I'm a loser. Everything I do is wrong. Let me ask you this: You never did *anything* right? Come on. Life has its ups and downs. No one is 100 percent right all of the time, and no one is 100 percent wrong all of the time. Thomas Edison, the greatest inventor in history, failed more than six hundred times in his experiments before he got it right. Even though he failed that many times, did that make him wrong? Or when he finally got it right, did that make him right 100 percent of the time? Of course not. Persistence is the key to success. You only fail when you stop trying to better yourself.

DISSING PERSON:

Are you disrespecting yourself with your own criticism? Are you disrespecting yourself by not accepting and believing positive feedback from others? Just because you believe something negative about yourself, it doesn't make it true. Is everyone else who compliments you wrong? Why not check out the facts about what they are telling you? I dare you to see if there is any truth to them. And if you are accepting the disrespectful words that other people who don't like you (or some who do) are saying, I dare you to check out their possible motivation. Look for the facts, and you will find the answers.

GUILTY PERSON:

I needed to do this . . . I should have done that . . . coulda, shoulda, woulda, etc. Didn't you make the choice you made because you thought it was the best one for you at the time? And wasn't it based on the way you felt at that time? Think about what were the motivating factors that led you to the decisions that you feel guilty about. And stop "coulda, shoulda, woulda." Living in the past only works if you're dead.

PROJECTOR PERSON:

You project a negative future for yourself. How can you tell what the future will hold for you? What facts do you have to support how your life will be in one, two or even five years from now? The only thing for certain is the uncertainty of the future.

PSYCHIC PERSON:

I feel it, so it must be true. Are you psychic? If you think you are, I dare you to check it out. Get a deck of cards, shuffle them, then place them face down. Now, use your psychic powers to tell me what card is on the top of the deck. After you have decided, based on your feelings, pick the card off the top of the deck and see if you are right. Do this until you go through fifty-two cards. Keep track of how many times you are right and how many times you are wrong. Feelings aren't always facts.

GOD PERSON:

I have complete power over myself and others. I am responsible for everything that is bad or has gone wrong in my life. I made people treat me in a negative or abusive way. Do you really have that kind of godly power? If so, I would like to meet you and get some lottery numbers. What about other people in your life, especially older people who were or are legally and morally responsible for you? What do you think about their decisions and choices that have affected your life? What was, or is, their motivation?

A CASUAL OBSERVER MAY NOTICE that some of these descriptions overlap, but it is very important what the child picks. From that we can see what their underlying concerns are about themselves. We then discuss whatever the children picked to describe their negative truth about themselves, and then we "Dare" them to write the real truth in another box at the bottom of the page—after they've deciphered what type of person they are and what may be the underlying causes for their negative feelings.

This self-help exercise can be done easily enough in the home by your own children. Sit and talk with them and spend some time working through the exercise. You, as a parent, may be amazed at what your child says and it will probably be just as amazing for the child to confront his or her own feelings and talk about them. After this is learned, kids can do it for themselves, and should be encouraged to do so.

That, by and large, is where the challenge of building self-worth begins—in self-awareness. When we are truly aware of the situations, facts, and problems facing us, we are able to make decisions that will increase our self-esteem and steer us away from the path of self-destruction.

CHAPTER 16
Prevention

"I'd love to nip any problems I see with my children in the bud, before they become serious. How, using these guidelines, can I do so?"

THE GOAL OF THIS BOOK HAS BEEN TO HELP PARENTS prevent serious problems with their children, particularly in the area of low self-esteem, abuse, and addiction. If a parent judiciously applies what we've talked about to their daily lives, we believe a parent can have a positive and critical impact on a child's development.

This final chapter will give a basic outline of what parents can do to effectively help their children. Positive parental guidance, and even the desire to abort any potential problems, is a big step in keeping things under control. It's all part of the necessary awareness and understanding, many aspects of which we've covered in this book.

When implementing what we've talked about, parents must employ patience when dealing with their children. Don't expect immediate results, and don't expect a dramatic turnaround. Parents who have gone from ignoring their child to suddenly getting involved in their child's life can, indeed, expect a lot of fighting, arguments, and resistance from their child. Stay the course. On one level the child may resent an apathetic parent who has suddenly become an interested parent, and may even question the motive behind the change in behavior. But on another level they want and need the attention.

It is critical to refrain from yelling. A stern, authoritative voice is completely different from a wild, shrill, uncontrollable yell. Get used to being stern, but not loud. The child may not respond right away.

Get used to it. And if for some reason the child doesn't respond verbally, he or she may respond better in writing.

Parents have had success in the past by encouraging their children to write down their feelings and emotions. Other parents have had success in writing down and posting on a wall a list of behaviors that a child is expected to exhibit. One of the finest examples of this was in a Tae-Kwan-Do class my son attended. Here is the list that we posted on his bedroom door.

Children are expected to:

1. Greet their parents with "Hi, Mom! Hi Dad!" when they enter the house. They should tell their parents "Good-bye!" when they leave.
2. Children will always be respectful of their parents, teachers, and other adults.
3. Children will be kind to their brothers and sisters.
4. Children will keep the house neat and clean.
5. Children will keep their hair, body, and teeth clean every day.
6. Children will not interrupt adult conversations.
7. Children will do these four things when they come home from school every day:
   A. Open the refrigerator and have a glass of milk or juice.
   B. Open your books to review what you have studied today.
   C. Do your homework.
   D. Preview what you are studying tomorrow.

Parents can also write down "Chore Charts" outlining what children are expected to do around the house on a daily basis and assign check marks or stars upon completion of the tasks.

All of these should be employed or tried out as the parent works to modify the child's behavior and harness the child's energy.

But, whatever is done, it should be done with the aforementioned patience and understanding. This is a critical step and hard to do.

When you show understanding, you must not simply give in to what the child wants nor should you dismiss or reward bad behavior under the guise of "understanding." Rather, you should seek to learn what feelings and motivations are behind a child's actions and then act to modify those actions accordingly. Understanding takes a degree of listening and learning from your child's behavior, and to modify his or her behavior takes action. Thus understanding is not a passive thing nor is it permissive.

Listening, a key component to understanding, is also neither passive nor permissive. You can't just hear what your child has to say, you must listen to the subtext of what the child is saying and mirror it back to the child.

"People hate me," says your child. "People hate you. Is that what you're saying?" you ask your child. "Why do you think people hate you?" Do not dismiss a child's opinion as invalid even if you believe it to be so. Rather, in listening to your child you will come to understand why your child feels the way he or she does. When you repeat what the child says back to the child, you're validating or discussing it in another way so the child feels that this "reflective listening" indicates true love and understanding.

Tough love is perhaps the most difficult concept to embrace for a mother and a father, but it is essential in the development of the child and integral to keep from rewarding negative behavior. It could be something as simple as keeping to a preordained punishment brought on by bad behavior. For example, let's say you've told your child that if he or she brings home bad grades without trying his hardest in class you are going to take away the child's telephone and television privileges. The child does in fact bring home bad grades with a comment from the teacher, "Doesn't listen in class. Refuses to try." Instead of following through on the punishment, you decide to back down. There are no consequences and the child learns that the parent is a paper tiger. The child is always testing the parent and may resent the boundaries you impose during childhood, but will grow to respect them and even want them.

The flip side of the tough love and discipline dynamic is the nurturing dynamic. A parent must learn to be supportive, where warranted, of attempts the child makes to make decisions for himself or herself and at the same time must put in time with the child to enable him to make good choices. There is no such thing as "quality time." Forget it. There is only quantity. The quality will come from the quantity. You cannot force tons of "quality time" into an insufficient quantity. If you have had children be prepared to sacrifice for them, and part of that has to be spending more time with them. This concept is extremely difficult and unpopular among upwardly mobile parents who are forever trying to climb corporate ladders of success. They forget what the child needs and why they are parents in the first place. It is not that they are necessarily apathetic, but rather they are harried. America today suffers from far too many harried parents. The single parent has the toughest row to hoe in this regard, but nonetheless must strive to support the children.

Any good prevention will include being on the lookout for self-sabotaging behavior. Usually when there is a problem between father and son or between mother and daughter we find that the children engage in this self-sabotaging behavior. The closer they get to success the surer they are to fail. They've been told for so long through deeds and words that they are no good that the child will struggle to make that come true.

Therefore when a parent witnesses self-sabotaging behavior on the part of a son or a daughter, the same-gender parent must reevaluate his or her own behavior. Are you as a parent being hypercritical? Rather than being supportive, are you constantly telling your child in so many words that they are not good enough? Are you trying to be supportive as a parent but always feel that your child is letting you down? Could it be that you are unconsciously dictating your child's failure by harsh and unkind words? These things must be considered in order to prevent a lowering of self-esteem and to keep depression and abuse at bay.

On the other hand, parents who engage in this behavior who are not of the same gender as their child can cause children to be fearful of failure to the point that they drive for success at the cost of everything else. These children are never satisfied with a B+ when they can get an A. They are never happy being in the top 5 percent of the class when they could be at the top. Something nice to strive for, one may think, but actually some of these children may be among the most unhappy and the most critical of themselves.

Getting your child involved in sports is yet another way to help prevent depression and combat low self-esteem. Not everyone is going to be a star, and you must take the time to find the right athletic program for your child, or else sports can also have a detrimental effect on your child's self-esteem. Interview prospective coaches and find out what the philosophy of the sports program is, and if it is something in which you wish your child to participate. A sports program that cuts children who aren't good enough, or one in which all the emphasis is placed on winning may not be the best place for children unsure of themselves. Find, instead, a program that teaches the fundamentals of the sport and preaches the concepts of fair play, good sportsmanship, and fun. Let the child have some fun and see the benefits in being a part of a team. Let them know there are things to which they can belong that are more important and larger than themselves. In this way the children will begin to feel better about themselves, you will instill confidence in them, and it will be a joy as a parent to see them play.

That, of course, is important too. As a parent, get involved in your child's activities. Sporting events can be as much fun for the parent as for the child.

There is yet another way parents can help their children become aware of things larger than themselves: God—in whatever form the family wishes to worship. How cynical we have become in this day and age to dismiss the wonders of the world, and how much solace can be obtained by reading, studying, and worshiping. Children naturally, in the course of growing up, have deep thoughts and questions about powers higher than themselves. It can enhance self-esteem and confidence to give the child the means to search for answers. Parents should take the time to discuss religion and God with their child when the child asks questions. At the same time the parent should be keen about getting the child involved in a greater community of worship at a young age and give them some grounding in a belief system.

There are other ways a parent can assist in preventing low self-esteem. We all need to learn from failure. Everyone fails. It's that simple. At some point everyone has tried to accomplish some task and not done it to his or her own satisfaction or to the satisfaction of others. But we like to say that no one truly fails until you stop trying. Keep trying. If you're not successful at one thing, then try another. Even if you aren't doing well, it doesn't mean you're a failure.

You'll find something you're good at. Also learn that it is a natural thing not to be perfect at everything. It doesn't and shouldn't destroy your self-esteem if your efforts are less than perfect. We're all less than perfect. We learn from our mistakes.

Another way to prevent problems with self-esteem and abuse is through education and reading. This does not necessarily mean education and reading about abuse and self-esteem problems. Literature, be it J.D. Salinger or William Shakespeare or anyone else, can help put a troubled mind in touch with other souls who've had problems. The wonderful thing about literature is that it can help children understand they are not alone. This refrain, universal in children since perhaps the beginning of time, is one of the hardest things to confront for a parent: "You don't understand. Nobody is like me." It is a powerful force that shuts out the rest of the world and keeps children from doing well. A proper education can combat this, as can the world of literature

When I was younger if I ever went to my parents and complained I was bored I invariably got a book thrust under my nose and was told that idle hands were the devil's tools and so I should go read. While that may seem extreme, the more learned and literate a child is, the better off he will be and the better armed to combat depression and low self-esteem.

Socialization is also a big factor in prevention. Children have to learn which places are conducive to helping their self-esteem and which are not. They need to stay away from people and places that can contribute to substance abuse. For example, hanging out at the local library would be a low-risk environment, whereas hanging out on the street corner with crack dealers would place your child at high risk. But it isn't just that black and white. Children have to learn how to handle themselves in the gray areas where both high-risk and low-risk behavior are carried on. The local skating rink may be a place where your son and daughter can get a good physical workout in a half-pipe, but it may also be a place where Ecstasy can be traded or you can find someone working out on a crack pipe. There are many places like that in today's society: the local mall, the book store, the movies, and even popular restaurants that serve as hang-outs for teens and other adolescents.

How you teach your children to interact and how much knowledge you impart about the dangers of drug abuse can have a positive impact on your child. It needs to go deeper than the slogan "Just Say No." That's a nice place to start, but the socialization of the child also has to include teaching the child to have some backbone and self-respect. That is key in getting children to make the right decisions for themselves.

Parents can cut down on the possibilities of socialization with questionable people, but never totally eliminate it. You can get your child involved in sports, or a poetry group, or a drama group, or a chess club or enrolled in an art class. These may be great, but no activity and no social setting is totally safe. The trick is to get your child to socialize and contribute to society in a positive manner so they can feel good about themselves and what they are doing for the greater good.

ACCEPTANCE, LOVE, AND APPROVAL. These are, at the core, what every child is looking for from a parent and what a parent needs to communicate to his or her child. Even if the children do something bad, the parent must let them know that they, the children, are still accepted. The behavior must change, but the children need to know that they are still loved. Actions may not be approved, but again, parents need to let their children know they approve of them as human beings.

The need to be loved and accepted are strong, driving forces in every human being and unless dealt with correctly can be twisted into the most bizarre and dangerous behaviors. One hesitates to draw an analogy with those who commit atrocious acts of sabotage and terrorism, but one can't help but wonder about the motivation behind such actions and the self-esteem of those who willingly engage in such behavior. It doesn't take much to think that Oklahoma City bomber Timothy McVeigh's life would have taken a different course if he had been exposed to different stimuli.

So let your children know you are happy with who they are— even if they're not the best athletes or the best students, as long as they are trying their hardest at everything they do.

SELF-ACCEPTANCE IS THE PRIMARY GOAL. Behind all of the preventative measures a parent may take, the idea is to produce children of strong character who accept themselves and can stand against the pressures of society. Self-acceptance is a goal that many adults haven't achieved and in many cases it boils down to the behaviors the adults themselves learned as children.

As vigilant parents we must be cognizant of our own problems, failings, and prejudices, and strive hard to keep our children from inheriting the worst in us.

A parent who is truly conscious of his or her own behavior in relationship to a child is a valuable commodity, an investment in our future, and one who can help make a great difference in today's complex and dangerous world.

A child who is cognizant of that fact can also be invaluable in today's world. Children are usually very perceptive and in my case they have proven to be far better children than I have been a parent. With that said, I offer you this essay from my oldest son. He was requested by his teacher to write an essay about the person who has influenced him the most in his life. Many of those in his class wrote about sports figures, presidents, actors, or historical figures.

This was what my son wrote.

INFLUENCE

The person who has influenced my life this year is not one person but two. You see, because these people are my best friends in the whole world! These people have helped me with my homework every year that I have been in school. This is possible because I have known them ever since I was born. I also know I can count on them when I know I can't count on anybody else. When I need to talk they are always there for me, and when I need help with just anything they are always there for me.

They are so close to me and I know them so well that sometimes I think that I have known them in another life in another time. They are so kind and helpful to me that when trying to describe this I am at a loss of words.

Another great thing about these people is that they are not always sweet and nice to me. This might sound bad but it is not because from this I have learned respect and discipline and I have learned to be kind to people even if I don't like them. Last but definitely not least I have learned patience.

There is only one thing left to say about these people and that is that they did not help me on this essay. This is good though because this essay is about them, and these people are my parents. ■

INDEX